D1717136

TECHNOLOGY IN ANCIENT CULTURES

ANCIENT

WARFARE

TECHNOLOGY

FROM JAVELINS TO CHARIOTS

Michael Woods and
Mary B. Woods

Twenty-First Century Books · Minneapolis

SOMERSET CO. LIBRARY
BRIDGEWATER, N.J. 08807

To Peg Goldstein, Greg Hunter, and Anna Cavallo

Copyright © 2011 by Michael Woods and Mary B. Woods

All rights reserved. International copyright secured. No part of this book may be reproduced, stored in a retrieval system, or transmitted in any form or by any means—electronic, mechanical, photocopying, recording, or otherwise—without the prior written permission of Lerner Publishing Group, Inc., except for the inclusion of brief quotations in an acknowledged review.

Twenty-First Century Books
A division of Lerner Publishing Group, Inc.
241 First Avenue North
Minneapolis, MN 55401 U.S.A.

Website address: www.lernerbooks.com

Library of Congress Cataloging-in-Publication Data

Woods, Michael, 1946-
    Ancient warfare technology : from javelins to chariots / by Michael Woods and Mary B. Woods.
        p.   cm. – (Technology in ancient cultures)
    Includes bibliographical references and index.
    ISBN 978–0–7613–6525–9 (lib. bdg. : alk. paper)
        1. Military art and science—History—To 500—Juvenile literature. 2. Military history, Ancient—Juvenile literature.
    3. Weapons, Ancient—Juvenile literature. 4. Military weapons, Ancient—Juvenile literature. I. Woods, Mary B.
    (Mary Boyle), 1946- II. Title.
    U29.W66 2011
    355.0209'01—dc22   2010031147

Manufactured in the United States of America
1 – PC – 12/31/10

TABLE OF CONTENTS

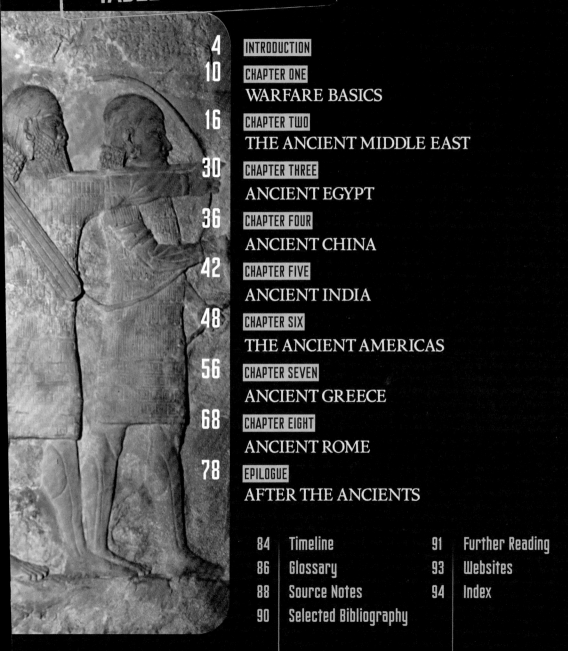

THE ANCIENT WORLDS OF WARFARE

BRITAIN

London

EUROPE

FRANCE

SPAIN

Rome

Syracuse

Carthage

MACEDONIA

Sparta

Troy
Athens

Hellespont

Mediterranean Sea

Jericho

EGYPT

ANCIENT
GREECE

MESOPOTAMIA

PERSIAN
EMPIRE

ASIA

CENTRAL
ASIA

GREAT
WALL

ANCIENT
INDIA

ANCIENT
CHINA

ROMAN
EMPIRE

ANCIENT
EGYPT

— Nile
R.

AFRICA

INDIAN OCEAN

ATLANTIC
OCEAN

AUSTRALIA

INTRODUCTION

What do you think of when you hear the word *technology*? You probably think of something totally new. You might think of research laboratories with computers, powerful microscopes, and other scientific tools. But technology doesn't refer to just brand-new machines and discoveries. Technology is as old as human society.

ANCIENT INDIA
ROMAN EMPIRE
ANCIENT GREECE
ANCIENT CHINA
ANCIENT EGYPT
ANCIENT MIDDLE EAST
INCA EMPIRE
⚘ Ancient site
• City

NORTH AMERICA

GREAT PLAINS

PACIFIC OCEAN

Tenochtitlán ⚘
AZTEC EMPIRE

CENTRAL AMERICA

ATLANTIC OCEAN

Amazon R.

Cusco
INCA EMPIRE

SOUTH AMERICA

Technology is the use of knowledge, inventions, and discoveries to make life better. The word *technology* comes from two Greek words. One, *techne*, means "art" or "craft." The other, *logos*, means "logic" or "reason." To the ancient Greeks, technology meant a discussion of arts and crafts. In modern times, the word usually refers to a craft, a technique, or a tool itself.

People use many kinds of technology. Medicine is one kind of technology. Transportation and agriculture are also kinds of technologies. This book looks at a form of technology that has helped people survive attacks by enemies and expand their political, social, and economic influence. That technology is warfare, or military, technology.

LIFE OR DEATH

Military technology involves the use of machines and techniques in warfare. But one of the most important kinds of military technology is knowledge. When generals draw up plans for using weapons and soldiers on the battlefield, they are using military technology.

Human beings have probably always used warfare to settle differences. In fact, much of the history of ancient times involves big battles and famous warriors. Military strength meant life or death to ancient societies. Conquering armies took over defeated territories. Conquering soldiers sometimes killed or enslaved the people they defeated.

In ancient times, new technology was often used for military purposes. For instance, when people first learned to make strong metals, such as bronze and iron, they immediately used these metals to make weapons.

▲ Assyrian warriors attack an enemy village in this relief carving from the palace of King Tiglath-pileser III (745–727 B.C.) in modern-day northern Iraq. Civilizations that held the advantage in warfare technology could conquer vast empires.

LEARNING ABOUT ANCIENT WARFARE

Ancient people left us a lot of information about armies, battles, and weapons. Many ancient writers recorded military history. Ancient artists often made sculptures and drawings of warriors. Some ancient weapons were made of wood, animal bone, and other natural materials. Most of

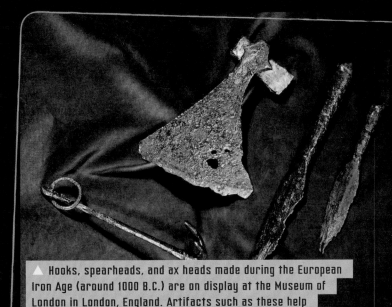

▲ Hooks, spearheads, and ax heads made during the European Iron Age (around 1000 B.C.) are on display at the Museum of London in London, England. Artifacts such as these help archaeologists learn about technology in ancient cultures.

these weapons decayed long ago. But other ancient weapons were made of metal. Modern-day scholars can study these weapons to learn how, when, and where they were used. Many ancient military forts were built of stone. Some of these structures are still standing, and historians can study them.

Sometimes it takes a little digging to find out about ancient warfare and other ancient technology. Around the world, ancient peoples built houses, storage sheds, and military forts, but these structures didn't last forever. In many cases, war, earthquakes, or storms damaged buildings. Or buildings simply fell down after many years of use. People hauled away the old wood, brick, or stone and constructed new buildings where the old ones had stood. Only the foundations from the original buildings remained. In other cases, people abandoned their settlements for places with more food or places that were more easily defended. Their old houses and other buildings eventually collapsed. Winds blew dirt into the structures.

Crumbling walls are all that remain of the Eurialo Castle, built by Dionysius the Elder (405–367 B.C.) at the Greek colony of Syracuse. The structure helped protect the colony from foreign invaders.

Rainstorms filled them with more dirt and mud. Plants grew over the newly deposited layers of earth. Eventually, houses and even whole ancient towns were buried and forgotten.

That's where archaeologists come in. Archaeologists are scientists who study the remains of past cultures. Often they have to dig through layers of earth to find traces of ancient structures. Sometimes they unearth entire ancient buildings. More often, only portions of the buildings remain. At excavation (digging) sites, archaeologists often find the remains of ancient military technology. They find stone spears, ancient armor, and defensive walls.

A LOT WITH A LITTLE

Ancient armies did not have stealth bombers, nuclear submarines, or spy satellites. Ancient weapons were simple. Most ancient soldiers fought with spears, daggers, and bows and arrows. Yet these simple weapons could be very destructive. In ancient wars, tens of thousands of men might die in a single battle. Sometimes ancient armies destroyed whole cities and conquered entire empires. Read on and discover how ancient warriors fought—and sometimes even changed the course of history.

CHAPTER ONE

WARFARE BASICS

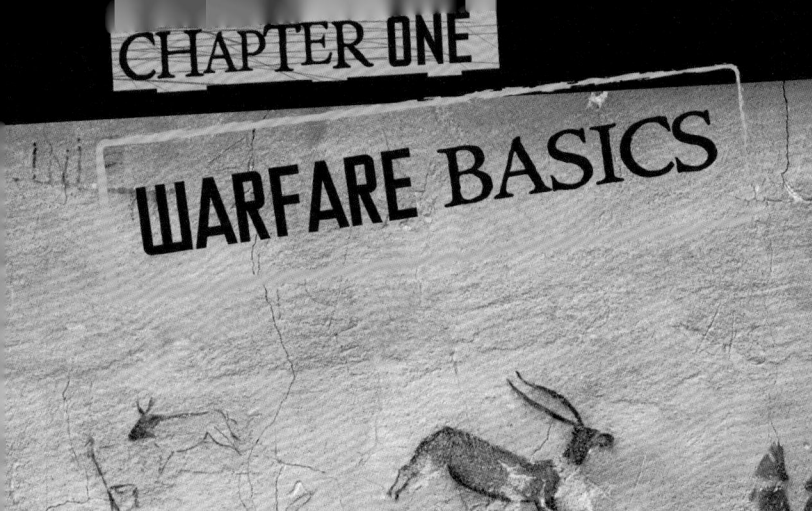

▲ Between fifteen and twenty thousand years ago, hunter-gatherers made these pictures of people and animals on the walls of a cave near Montignac, France. Ancient hunter-gatherers used spears, throwing sticks, slings, and arrows to kill animals and sometimes to kill one another.

The first humans on Earth lived about 2.5 million years ago. They were hunters and gatherers. They lived in small groups and got their food by hunting game, fishing, and gathering wild plants. When the food in one area was all used up, the group moved to a new place. Hunter-gatherers made tools from stone, wood, animal bones, plant fibers, and clay. In some places on Earth, the hunter-gatherer lifestyle remained unchanged until only a few centuries ago.

STICKS AND STONES

Early humans made knives and axes by knapping, or knocking rocks together. They used one rock to break flakes off another, leaving the second stone with a sharp edge. Early humans made spears from long straight sticks, with stone spearheads attached to the end. They made clubs from wood and animal bone. People used these tools to hunt animals.

People probably used these same tools to kill one another. Archaeologists think that early humans sometimes fought over food and territory. They probably used their hunting weapons against rival groups.

These arrowheads from ancient Peru are six to eight thousand years old. Ancient hunters used flint, jasper, and other kinds of stones to make arrowheads and other weapons.

NEW TECHNOLOGY

As the centuries passed, ancient peoples developed new hunting tools. One was the spear-thrower. This device was a simple stick, a little shorter than a man's arm. The front end of the spear-thrower rested in a hunter's hand, along with the spear. When the hunter released the spear, the back end of the spear-thrower pushed the spear forward with extra force. With a spear-thrower, a human hunter could propel a spear four times farther than he could with muscle power alone. The oldest known spear-throwers come from caves in France. They date to around 15,000 to 11,000 B.C.

Like spear-throwers, slings allowed ancient hunters to launch missiles with more force than they could with only muscle power. In the case of the sling, the missile was a simple stone. When fired from a sling, a stone could be deadly. A sling was made from two leather cords fastened to a leather pouch. The hunter put a small stone in the pouch, held both cords, and whirled the device overhead. At just the right instant, he released one of the cords. The stone shot toward its target.

Another simple hunting tool was the throwing stick. This weapon was just what the name says—a stick thrown through the air. Unlike spears, which flew straight, throwing sticks spun end over end in flight. A well-thrown stick could kill a rabbit, a bird, or another small animal. Most throwing sticks were made of wood, but hunters also made them from animal bones and tusks.

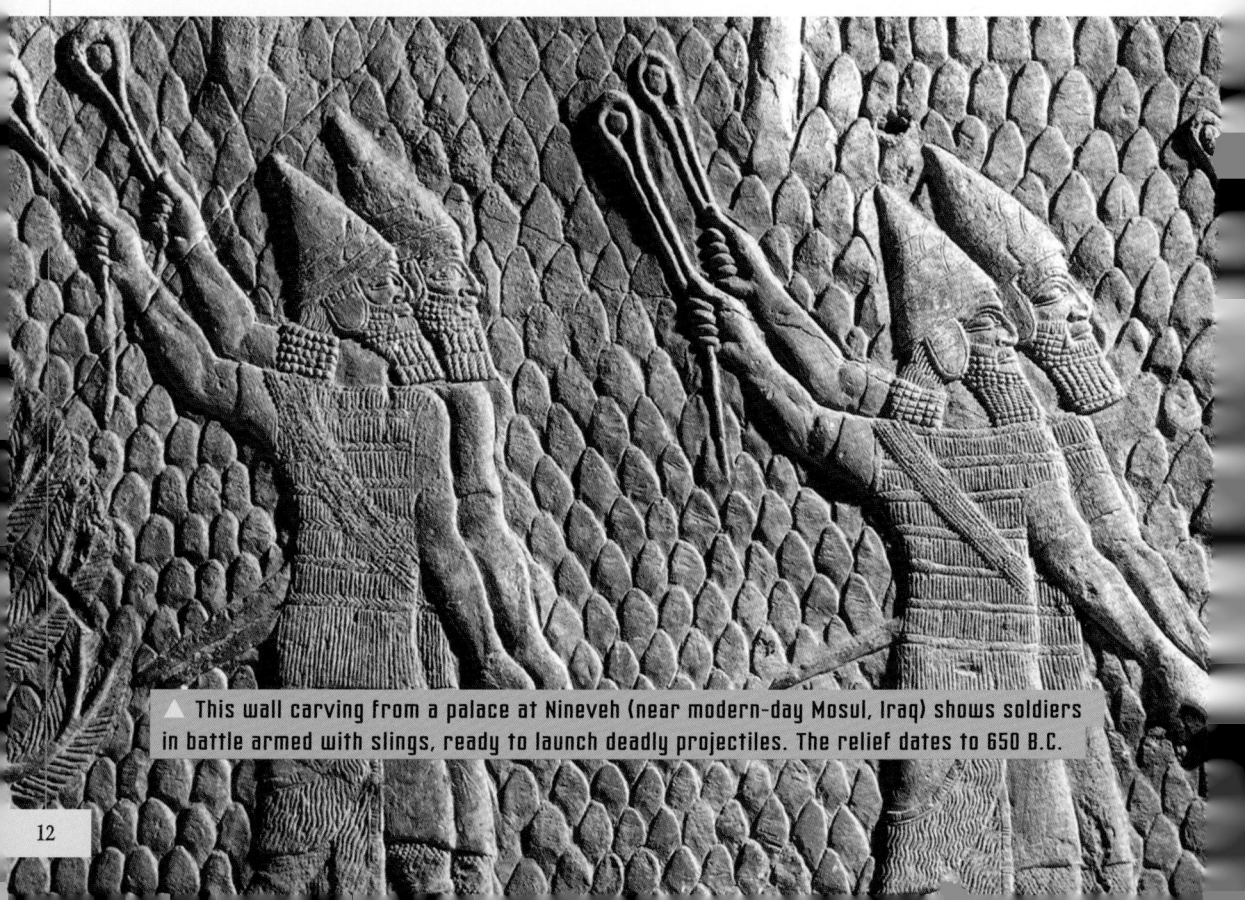

▲ This wall carving from a palace at Nineveh (near modern-day Mosul, Iraq) shows soldiers in battle armed with slings, ready to launch deadly projectiles. The relief dates to 650 B.C.

RETURN TO SENDER

Boomerangs *(shown in this cave art from northwestern Australia)* come in two types: returning and nonreturning. Both types are curved, flat sticks. But returning boomerangs have a sharper, more V-shaped curve. This special shape allows returning boomerangs to fly through the air and return to the spot from which they

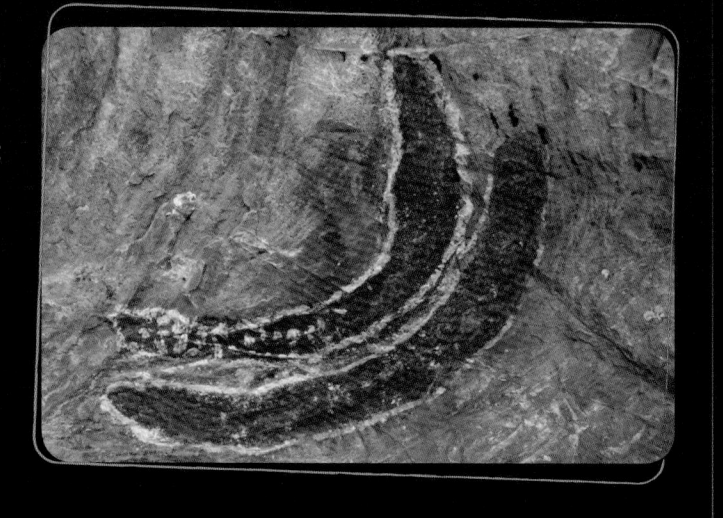

were thrown. Ancient Australians invented returning boomerangs. In flight they looked like birds of prey. Australian hunters used them to frighten or trick game birds.

Eventually hunters discovered that flat, curved throwing sticks flew farther than round, straight ones. They hit their targets with more force. Their winglike design helped the sticks stay aloft. Hunters began to fashion flat, curved throwing sticks, which are called boomerangs. Most people associate boomerangs with ancient Australia. They were widely used there, and the name *boomerang* comes from Australia. But ancient peoples in other parts of the world also used boomerangs.

"The history of the sword is the history of humanity."

—British explorer Richard Burton, 1884

Spear-throwers, slings, throwing sticks, and boomerangs all made hunting easier and more efficient. And once people had learned to kill animals with these tools, they realized they could use them against human enemies. A cave painting from northern Australia shows what might be the first-ever battle scene. The painting shows warriors holding spears, boomerangs, and clubs. Some of the soldiers stoop to help injured comrades, who have spears sticking out of their bodies. The painting is more than ten thousand years old, but ancient peoples were probably fighting with one another thousands of years before that.

ANCIENT ARCHERS

We do not know who invented the bow and arrow or when, but the invention was a big breakthrough in both ancient hunting and ancient warfare. Early hunters made bows from pieces of flexible wood, such as elm, ash, or yew. They made a bowstring from animal intestines, flax, or another fiber. The bowstring connected one end of the bow to the other. It pulled the two ends of the bow toward each other, so the bow was slightly curved.

To operate the weapon, an archer held the bow in one hand. He drew back the bowstring and an arrow with the other hand. The archer's pull increased the bend

▲ This rock carving from Sweden is about three thousand years old. It shows a hunter with a bow and arrow. Bows and arrows were effective weapons for both hunting and warfare.

of the bow. When the archer let go of the bowstring, the bow sprung back to its original shape. This quick unbending of the bow propelled the arrow forward.

The first arrows were made from strong reeds or tree branches. Finding the right branch was important, because only a perfectly straight arrow would fly straight. Arrows were usually about half the length of bows. The weight of an arrow was also important. A light arrow would fly the farthest but had less power to penetrate, or pierce, its target. A heavy arrow had great penetration power but would not fly very far.

At first, arrow makers simply sharpened one end of an arrow to make a point. The other end was notched to fit the bowstring. Later, arrow makers learned to harden the points of arrows by heating them in a fire. Then hunters realized that an arrowhead, made of a sharp piece of stone, would help the arrow cut and pierce its target. Arrows with good heads penetrated flesh deeply and killed quickly. With arrowheads, the bow and arrow became the world's most deadly weapon.

BAD SCENE

Ancient people used bows and arrows to kill animals and sometimes one another. Sudan, a modern country in north central Africa, has a burial ground called the Jebel Sahaba. The site dates from about 8000 B.C. Archaeologists have found fifty-eight skeletons at the site. The dead included many women and children. The archaeologists also found many arrowheads mixed in with the bones. Experts aren't sure what exactly happened at Jebel Sahaba. But it was probably the site of an ancient massacre with bows and arrows.

CHAPTER TWO

THE ANCIENT MIDDLE EAST

Around 10,000 B.C., people in the Middle East began to abandon the hunter-gatherer lifestyle. In a region called the Fertile Crescent, they began to raise crops and livestock. They settled into farming villages. Early farmers grew enough food for their families and sometimes even more food than they needed. When they had a surplus, they could sell or trade it.

Middle Eastern farmers needed systems for keeping track of crops, farmland, and money. They invented a writing system called cuneiform. They also created laws and governments. Rulers wanted to protect their territory, and they often wanted more territory, wealth, and power. For that, they needed weapons and armies.

▲ This limestone carving from Abu Simbel in southern Egypt dates to the thirteenth century B.C. The picture shows Hittite soldiers, who carry large, round shields for protection.

KING-GENERALS

Can you imagine the president of the United States leading troops into battle? In the modern world, that's a far-fetched idea. Modern leaders give the orders to fight, but they usually stay far away from the battlefield. But in ancient times, kings and other rulers did more than just give orders. They left their palaces and led armies to war. The greatest kings were the greatest generals. Many were skilled archers or horsemen.

The Assyrians, a Middle Eastern group, had some of the ancient world's most skilled king-generals. Assyrian rulers such as Tiglath-pileser III, Sargon II, and Sennacherib amassed armies of more than one hundred thousand soldiers. Then they led their troops in the field. By the 600s B.C., Assyria controlled a large portion of the ancient Middle East, from the Mediterranean Sea in the west to the Persian Gulf in the east.

This victory stela (carved stone slab) from about 2230 B.C. shows Akkadian king Naram-Sin trampling enemies beneath his feet. Ancient kings not only oversaw their kingdoms, but they also led troops in battle.

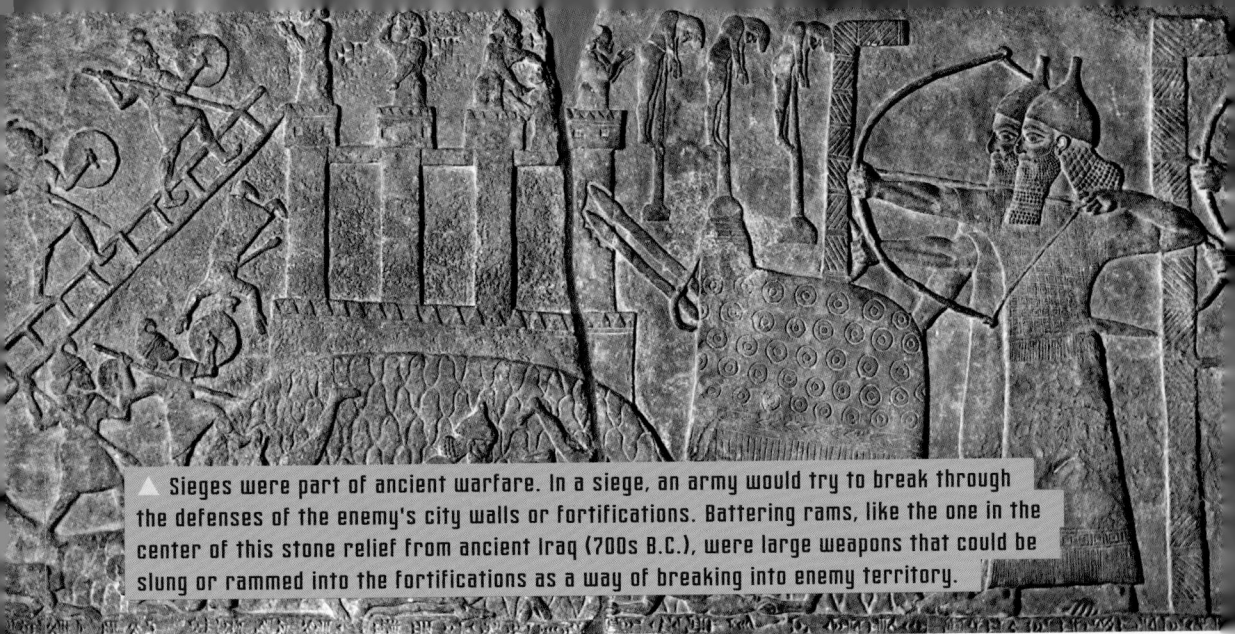

▲ Sieges were part of ancient warfare. In a siege, an army would try to break through the defenses of the enemy's city walls or fortifications. Battering rams, like the one in the center of this stone relief from ancient Iraq (700s B.C.), were large weapons that could be slung or rammed into the fortifications as a way of breaking into enemy territory.

ANCIENT DRAFT

Amassing a large army has never been easy. Many people don't want to join the army. After all, the job can get you killed. To solve this problem, many governments require people—especially young men—to join the army. The system of calling up people for military service is called a draft. It is not a new idea. Many ancient kingdoms drafted men into the army.

In the ancient kingdom of Mari, in modern-day Syria, the government required men to serve in the military. They were supposed to register for service at government offices. But despite the offer of free meals and gifts, many men refused to register. The officer in charge of registration proposed a solution to Zimri-Lim, Mari's king: "If my lord will agree, let me execute a criminal [a man who had refused to register] in the prison, cut off his head and parade it all around the town . . . to make men afraid so that they will assemble quickly." We don't know if Zimri-Lim agreed to the idea. But we do know that he was a very successful military leader who never lacked troops.

ENOUGH TO FEED AN ARMY

Imagine trying to feed an ancient army of one hundred thousand men three times a day. If each man ate 1 pound (0.5 kilograms) of bread a day, the army would need 50 tons (45 metric tons) of wheat daily. And these were hungry men,

This decorated box comes from Ur, a city in ancient Iraq, and dates to about 2500 B.C. The drawings show soldiers on the march. Ancient armies used four-wheeled carts to carry supplies. They used two-wheeled chariots in combat.

who sometimes marched or fought all day. How could ancient armies acquire the food they needed?

Armies transported some food supplies in wheeled carts. They also took along "self-transporting" food in the form of herds of cattle. The cattle marched with the army. They grazed on grass along the way. Soldiers slaughtered cows and ate them as necessary. But soldiers still needed more food.

To solve the problem, ancient Middle Eastern armies simply took what they needed from the lands they passed through. As soldiers marched, they picked crops, took livestock, and raided stockpiles of grain, beer, wine, olive oil, and other foods belonging to local people. Generals often scheduled campaigns at harvesttime, so that plenty of food would be available. The strategy had a terrible impact on civilians. They often starved after an army marched past.

MADE OF METAL

The first weapons were made from natural materials. These included rocks, bones, and sticks. Around 5000 B.C., people in the ancient Middle East began making weapons and other tools from copper. Copper is a soft metal. By heating and hammering copper, ancient craftspeople could easily shape it into swords, arrowheads, and other weapons.

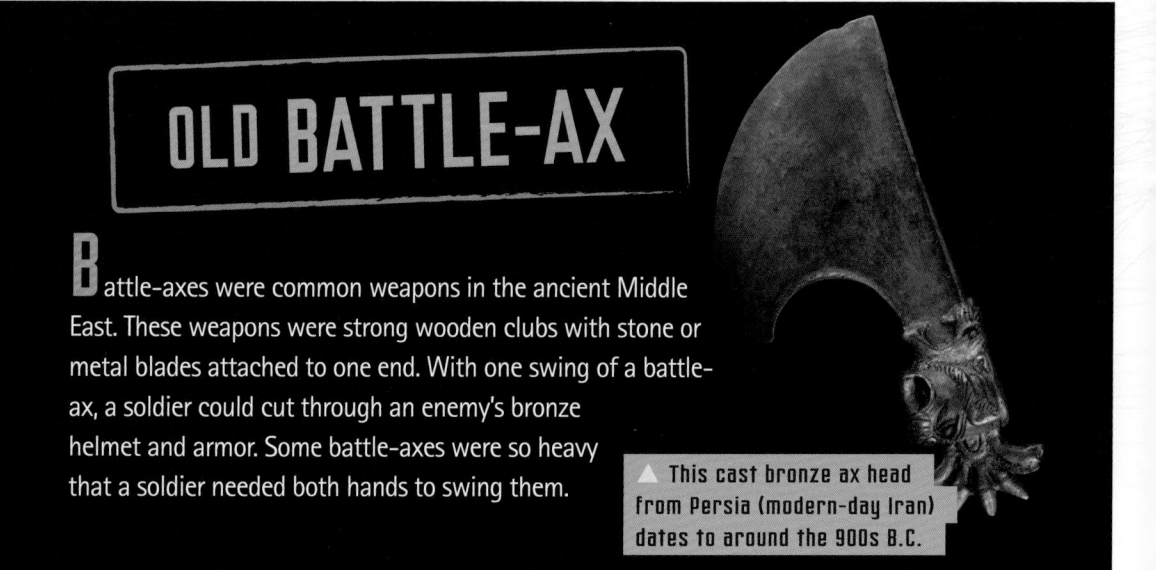

OLD BATTLE-AX

Battle-axes were common weapons in the ancient Middle East. These weapons were strong wooden clubs with stone or metal blades attached to one end. With one swing of a battle-ax, a soldier could cut through an enemy's bronze helmet and armor. Some battle-axes were so heavy that a soldier needed both hands to swing them.

▲ This cast bronze ax head from Persia (modern-day Iran) dates to around the 900s B.C.

Around 3000 B.C., Middle Eastern metalsmiths learned to make a harder metal. They melted copper and tin together in a hot furnace, then let the mixture cool and harden. The result was bronze. Bronze weapons did not bend or break as easily as copper ones. Copper blades often grew dull after repeated use. Bronze blades stayed sharp longer.

In about 1550 B.C., invaders from modern-day Turkey marched toward Mesopotamia, a region between the Tigris and Euphrates rivers in modern-day Iraq. These invaders were the Hittites. Other Middle Eastern groups feared them, and they quickly conquered Mesopotamia. The Hittites' power rested in their strong weapons. These weapons were made of iron, whereas other groups fought with bronze weapons. Although the Hittites tried to keep iron technology a secret, the information soon spread. Other groups began to make iron weapons, and the Hittites lost their military advantage.

WAR ON WHEELS

The earliest armies fought on foot. They marched until they neared the enemy. When they were within firing distance, archers shot at the enemy with bows and arrows. Other soldiers moved in with spears, daggers, battle-axes, and clubs for hand-to-hand combat.

In about 3000 B.C., new technology changed warfare in ancient Mesopotamia. That technology was the wheel. The wheel made armies and soldiers more mobile. Armies used wheeled carts to transport supplies. On the battlefield, armies used wheeled vehicles called chariots.

The ancient war chariot usually had two wheels. It was pulled by horses. Three soldiers staffed the vehicle. One drove, one shot arrows, and one held a shield to protect the archer and the driver. Soldiers in horse-drawn chariots could circle enemy foot soldiers and assail them with a shower of arrows. Foot soldiers were helpless against such an attack. Chariots moved too fast and were often too far away for foot soldiers to make a counterattack.

This Assyrian relief from the 600s B.C. shows war chariots in the bloody Battle of Til-Tuba in ancient Iraq. War chariots were light, open-wheeled vehicles pulled by horses. Charioteers drove the fast vehicles and protected themselves with shields.

After thinning the enemy ranks from a distance, charioteers would charge directly into the enemy army. This tactic usually scattered the enemy soldiers and broke their defensive formation. The charioteers continued their attack, while their army's foot soldiers moved in from another direction to further disrupt enemy defenses.

Before the introduction of chariots, military leaders who gathered the largest number of soldiers on a battlefield often won the battle. But chariots reduced the value of huge armies. Instead, the army with the most chariots and best-trained chariot crews had the edge.

Chariots did have disadvantages. They were expensive to build, and their crews required long training. Chariots were not effective in fighting on rough or rocky land, which could easily injure horses and damage vehicles and wheels. Chariots also required extra manpower, including the driver and shield bearer, plus men to care for and feed horses.

A BETTER BOW

Around the same time Mesopotamian armies began using chariots, they began using better bows. Instead of being made from a single strip of wood, they were made from a composite, or collection, of materials. They are called composite bows.

The bow's interior layer was a strip of strong, flexible wood. The bow maker glued a strip of animal horn along the inside curve of the bow. He glued strips of stretchy animal sinew, or tendons, along the outer curve. The glue that held the materials together was derived from substances inside animal bone and animal hide.

Pulling on the bowstring of a composite bow stretched the sinew at the front of the bow and compressed the animal horn at the back. When the string was released, both materials instantly sprung back into shape. This springing motion propelled arrows toward their targets with great speed and force.

▶ This stone carving from ancient Iraq shows Assyrian warriors shooting arrows. Composite bows, developed in Mesopotamia, helped archers shoot farther and with more force.

Composite bows were much more powerful than earlier bows. They could shoot arrows about two or three times farther. Composite bows were also shorter than earlier bows, so archers could easily fire them from the crowded interior of a chariot.

ARMED HORSEMEN

Originally, horses were not large animals like those of modern times. Most early horses were too small to ride in battle. But along with growing crops, early farmers also learned to breed animals. They mated male and female animals with desirable traits to produce offspring who also had those traits. For instance, the offspring of a large male horse and a large female horse would probably also be large. Over many centuries, horse breeders in Persia (modern-day Iran) and central Asia bred horses to be big, strong, and heavy. These new breeds of horses were well suited for warfare.

But big horses weren't enough. For stability on horseback, ancient horsemen needed stirrups and saddles. Stirrups made horses easier to mount. Without stirrups, riders had to vault onto horses. Only people in top physical condition could jump so high. Saddles gave riders improved balance from front to back. Stirrups added side-to-side balance. With a stirrup and a saddle, the horse and rider became a single stable unit. With his weight on

▲ Ancient cavalry (warriors on horseback) threw spears, shot arrows, and swung battle-axes while riding. This stone carving from the ancient palace (in modern-day Iraq) of Ashurbanipal, king of the Assyrians in the 600s B.C., shows armed horsemen.

the stirrups, a rider could carry a long spear, brace it firmly against his body, and charge an enemy. He could lift a heavy sword or battle-ax high above his head and slash down hard without losing his balance. He could even shoot arrows while riding. Archaeologists think that horsemen in central Asia were the first riders to use saddles. Ancient Indians were the first riders to use stirrups. Both kinds of technology then spread to the ancient Middle East.

Soldiers who fight on horseback are called cavalry. The Egyptians, Canaanites, and Assyrians were the first ancient peoples to use cavalry troops.

ON THE DEFENSIVE

The development of more lethal offensive weapons created the need for better defensive technology. This technology included armor, helmets, and shields. Soldiers of ancient Sumer (in modern-day Iraq) carried large rectangular shields. They protected the body from the neck to below the knees. A soldier held his shield with one hand and his weapon with the other. Shields were made of wood covered with layers of leather and cloth.

The first body armor was probably made of thick leather. One picture from Ur, an ancient Mesopotamian city, shows soldiers wearing leather capes. The capes would have offered a layer of protection against minor cuts and body blows. But they probably weren't much help against heavy blows.

> **"As the Philistine [warrior] moved closer to attack him, David ran quickly toward the battle line to meet him. Reaching into his bag and taking out a stone, he slung it and struck the Philistine on the forehead. The stone sank into his forehead, and he fell face-down on the ground. So David triumphed over the Philistine with a sling and a stone; without a sword in his hand he struck down the Philistine and killed him."**

—Hebrew Bible, first millennium (thousand years) B.C.

Assyrian soldiers wore tough leather garments that covered their bodies from chest to knees. Links of metal chain were sewn onto the leather. The metal provided protection against arrows and spears.

Images from ancient Assyria often show soldiers wearing cone-shaped hats. Made from cloth, leather, and metal, these were the first battle helmets. Because of the cone-shaped design, downward blows from a sword tended to glance off the helmets. A flap in back of the helmet protected the soldier's neck.

▲ Ancient soldiers protected themselves from enemy weapons with helmets, body armor, and shields, as depicted in this Assyrian carving from the 600s B.C.

CITY WALLS

Most ancient cities were surrounded by high walls. The walls were built for defense. They had watchtowers, where defenders could keep a lookout for attackers. They also contained elevated platforms from which defenders could fire at attackers. In addition, many ancient cities were built on hills or other high ground. High ground is easier to defend than low ground. High ground offers a good view of approaching enemies. And it is much harder to scramble uphill to attack an enemy than to shoot or run downhill toward an approaching enemy.

While defenders did their best to keep ancient cities safe, attackers did their best to get past city walls. Attackers tried to climb over walls with the help of ropes and ladders. They tried to knock down walls by ramming them with heavy wooden beams. Sometimes they even attempted to tunnel

▲ In this carving from ancient Iraq, dated to the mid-600s B.C., soldiers besiege (attack) an enemy city using ladders, bows and arrows, and other weapons.

under walls or burn through the city gates. These tactics were hit or miss. Sometimes they worked. Sometimes they didn't.

One tactic, first used in ancient Assyria, was superior to all others. It was called siege warfare. During a siege, soldiers surrounded a walled town so that enemy soldiers and citizens could not leave or enter. The attackers cut off supplies of food and other materials needed by townspeople. They tried to starve the enemy into surrender. The attackers also tried to wear down the defenders with repeated assaults on the city walls. If the attackers were patient enough, they might not have to fight at all. They just had to wait outside the city until food and water ran out inside. Then the defenders would have to surrender or die.

But sieges were not usually that simple. If defenders had advance notice of an enemy's approach, they could prepare for a siege. Townspeople could stockpile food. They could bring cattle and sheep inside the city walls to provide a supply of milk and meat. In addition, most cities had wells within their walls to supply water. Sometimes such preparations worked. After weeks or months, the besieging army would get frustrated, grow short on food itself, and go home.

THE OLDEST WALLED CITY

The first walled city known to archaeologists was Jericho, part of modern-day Israel. People built the city and its wall around 8000 B.C. The stone wall around the city contained a brick watchtower, from which guards could look out for enemies. Guards climbed a spiral staircase to reach the top of the tower.

GUERRILLA WARFARE

Guerrilla warfare involves small bands of soldiers who make quick, small-scale ambushes. In conventional warfare, large armies meet on the battlefield. But guerrillas avoid such confrontations. Instead, they operate secretly and at night. They usually don't wear military uniforms, so enemies can't distinguish them from ordinary citizens.

Guerrilla warfare might sound like a modern technique. But the ancient Scythians used guerrilla tactics more than twenty-five hundred years ago. The Scythians were nomads, or people who travel from place to place. They moved with herds of sheep, cattle, and horses around their home territory in modern-day Ukraine. In 513 B.C., Darius I, the king of Persia, invaded Scythian territory. Darius had the most powerful army in the world. But the Scythians resisted him by using guerrilla tactics. Small groups of Scythian horsemen approached Darius's army, but they never came near enough to fight. Instead, they retreated, luring Darius deeper and deeper into Scythian territory.

Eventually, Darius grew frustrated. He sent a message to the Scythian king: "If you think you can oppose my power, halt there and fight." Finally, small groups of Scythian horsemen began to attack Darius's soldiers. The Scythians ambushed the Persians at night. They also destroyed crops and water supplies that Darius's army relied on. Ultimately, the guerrilla tactics worked. Darius withdrew from Scythian territory. It never became part of his empire.

WHAT'S IN A NAME?

Although the ancient Scythians used guerrilla tactics, the term *guerrilla* wasn't coined until the early 1800s. The word means "little war" in Spanish.

BRIDGE TO SOMEWHERE

Darius's son Xerxes I ruled the Persian Empire in the 400s B.C. He wanted to conquer Greece, which also had been Darius's goal. In 480 B.C., Xerxes began his campaign against Greece. He needed to take his army across the Hellespont (the modern-day Dardanelles). This strait, or narrow body of water, separates modern-day Turkey from Europe. The strait is only 1 mile (1.6 kilometers) across at some spots. Xerxes ordered his engineers to build a bridge across the strait.

The engineers came up with a clever design. They positioned 676 ships side by side across the waterway. Soldiers stretched heavy wooden planks from ship to ship to make a road. The bridge enabled soldiers, vehicles, and animals to cross the Hellespont.

Despite this success, the Persians eventually lost their war with Greece. Persian nobles, disappointed in their leader, then murdered Xerxes.

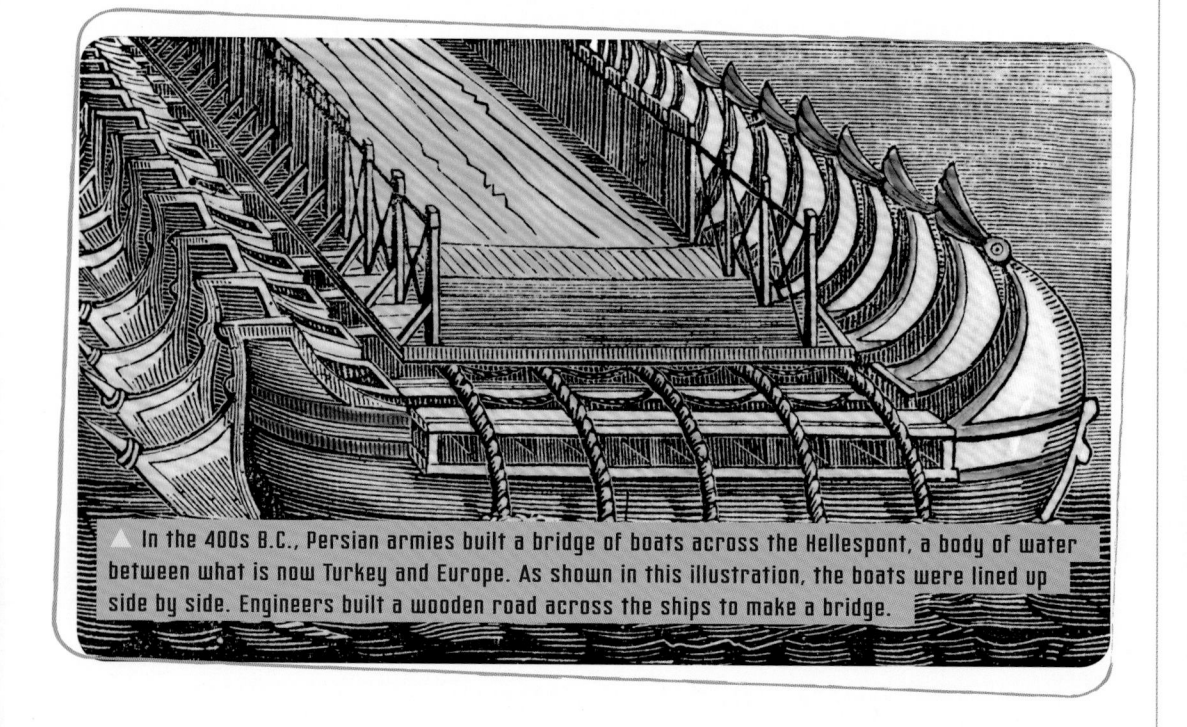

▲ In the 400s B.C., Persian armies built a bridge of boats across the Hellespont, a body of water between what is now Turkey and Europe. As shown in this illustration, the boats were lined up side by side. Engineers built a wooden road across the ships to make a bridge.

CHAPTER THREE

ANCIENT EGYPT

This photo shows the Nile River. The ancient Egyptians lived along the river and conquered nearby territories in northern Africa and the Middle East.

Around 5000 B.C., ancient hunter-gatherers began to settle around the Nile River in Egypt. People built permanent farms and villages along the river. They grew wheat and other crops.

Eventually, two kingdoms developed in Egypt. One kingdom (Lower Egypt) consisted of villages around the Nile Delta. This is the area where the river splits into branches and empties into the Mediterranean Sea. The other kingdom (Upper Egypt) consisted of villages south of the Nile Delta. Around 3100 B.C., Upper Egypt conquered Lower Egypt. The two kingdoms became one.

KING NARMER'S MACE

In 1897 archaeologists found a stone tablet in southern Egypt. Called the Narmer Palette, the tablet is covered with carvings on both sides. The carvings show people, animals, and weapons. Historians aren't sure what all the images mean, but most historians think the tablet depicts the conquest of Lower Egypt by Upper Egypt.

One side of the tablet shows Narmer, a king from Upper Egypt, smashing an enemy's head with a mace. A mace is a wooden club with a heavy stone attached to one end. Maces were common in ancient warfare. Soldiers swung maces to bash enemy fighters in close combat. Along with the Narmer Palette, archaeologists found a mace head (a stone from the end of a mace) marked with Narmer's name. The king probably didn't use this mace head in battle. Archaeologists think it was used only for ceremonies.

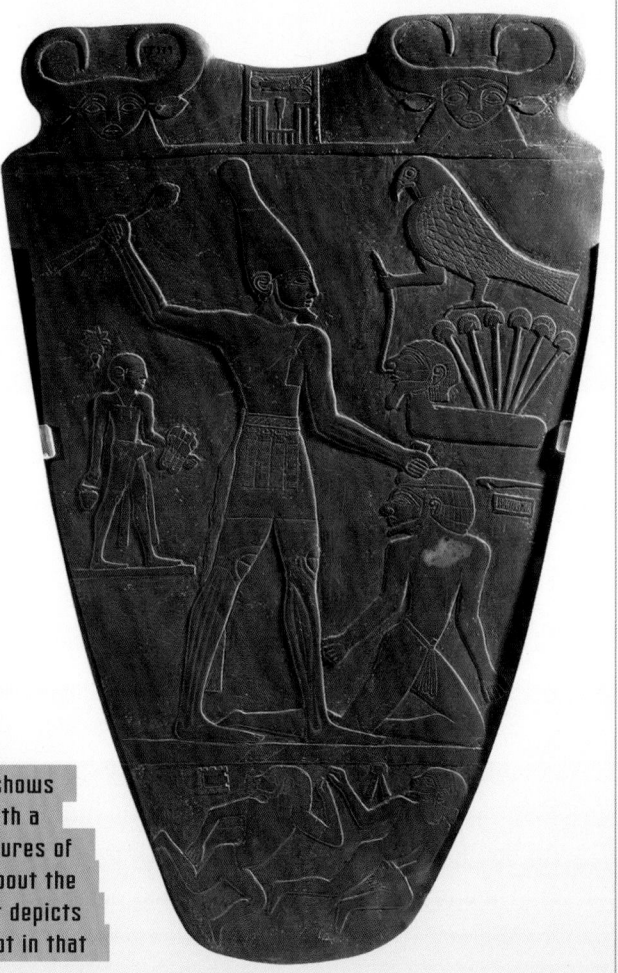

▶ One side of the Narmer Palette (right) shows Egyptian king Narmer striking an enemy with a club called a mace. The other side has pictures of people and animals. The palette dates to about the thirty-first century B.C. Historians think it depicts the conquest of Lower Egypt by Upper Egypt in that same century.

HAFTING TECHNOLOGY

Imagine an arrow with its head tied to the side of the shaft. The arrow would be unbalanced and would not fly straight. To work best, an arrowhead and its shaft need to be aligned directly end to end. Hafting is the process of attaching the head or point of a weapon to a shaft. In the ancient world, maces, battle-axes, spears, arrows, and other weapons all needed to be hafted properly to work well.

Ancient craftspeople developed several hafting techniques. One involved putting a tang, a small projecting tab, on the base of a spear or arrowhead. The tang fit into a slot at the end of the arrow or spear shaft. A cord tied tightly around the shaft constricted the slot. The tight slot held the tang in place.

Craftspeople used a similar technique to haft mace heads (above) to mace handles. The craftsperson drilled a hole into the stone mace head. He then pounded the handle firmly into the hole. The connection stayed tight, even after many swings.

SEA POWER

After unification, Egypt became rich and powerful. The kingdom had fertile farmland, copper mines, and other natural resources. Egyptian rulers amassed large armies to protect the kingdom and to invade nearby countries.

Egypt also built a powerful navy. Shipbuilders constructed strong wooden warships. These vessels were sturdy enough to sail on the Mediterranean Sea. The warships used both wind power and people power. Each side of a ship had a row of oars, pulled by oarsmen. The ship also had a square sail attached to a mast. Sailors took advantage of wind power when traveling on the open sea. But when it was time for battle, they switched to human power. They lowered the sail and pulled down the ship's mast to protect it from damage. Then oarsmen did the work of powering the ship.

A modern illustration of an Egyptian warship shows armed Egyptian soldiers on their way to battle. A sailor steers the ship with a big rudder located at the back, or stern, of the boat. Moving the rudder from side to side turns the boat to the left or the right.

Egyptian warships were well designed for fighting. High gunwales, the edges around the side of a ship, protected the oarsmen from enemy arrows. Raised platforms on the ship allowed archers to shoot their own arrows at the enemy. Some Egyptian warships had a ram on the front. Sailors used it to smash through the sides of enemy ships.

THE NAPOLEON OF EGYPT

Thutmose III, who ruled from 1479 to 1425 B.C., led Egypt to the height of its power. He was a brilliant military strategist, as well as a talented archer and horseman. Like other king-generals, he personally led his troops in battle. He rode at the head of a column of soldiers in a silver and gold chariot. Under his rule, Egypt conquered enemy kingdoms in modern-day Syria and Israel. It also conquered Nubia, an ancient kingdom south of Egypt.

Much of what we know about Thutmose comes from the Temple of Amun in the Egyptian city of Thebes (modern-day Luxor). The walls of the temple are covered with hieroglyphics, or picture writing. The writing details Thutmose's military exploits.

The hieroglyphics explain how Thutmose conquered Megiddo, near the modern-day city of Haifa, Israel. Two roads led toward the city. One was wide and smooth. The other was narrow, hilly, and rocky. Thutmose figured the enemy would expect him to march on the wide road, so he took his army over the narrow road. Meanwhile, most of the enemy soldiers waited at the end of the wide road. Thutmose arrived at the city with little resistance. His troop's easily defeated the city's defenders. His troops then went on to plunder the riches of Megiddo. They took hundreds of chariots, horses, bushels of grain, and prisoners of war.

▲ Carvings on the walls of the Temple of Amun in Egypt tell of the ancient military feats of Thutmose III. In this image, Thutmose defeats the Hittites in the 1400s B.C.

"Then the tents of His Majesty were pitched, and orders were sent out to the whole army, saying, Arm yourselves, get your weapons ready, for we shall set out to do battle with the miserable enemy at daybreak."

—description of the Battle of Megiddo, written on the walls of the Temple of Amun, 1400s or 1300s B.C.

After Megiddo, Thutmose won sixteen more military campaigns. His military skill earned him several nicknames. One is the Warrior Pharaoh, or king. Another is the Napoleon of Egypt. This nickname, bestowed thousands of years after Thutmose's death, refers to Napoleon Bonaparte, a power-hungry French emperor and general.

THE FIRST PEACE TREATY

Countries often end wars by signing peace treaties. These documents list the conditions under which all sides will stop fighting. The first written peace treaty that survives in full was made around 1270 B.C. In the agreement, the Egyptian ruler Ramses II and Hattusilis III, the king of the Hittites, agreed never to fight again. They agreed to send prisoners of war home and to help each other during future wars. The treaty reads in part:

> If a foreigner marches against the country of Egypt and if [Ramses], the great king, the king of the country of Egypt, your brother, sends to Hattusilis, the king of the country of Hatti [kingdom of the Hittites], his brother, the following message: "Come to my help against him," then Hattusilis, king of the country of Hatti, shall send his troops and his chariots and kill my enemy.

CHAPTER FOUR

ANCIENT CHINA

People built the first villages in China around 3000 B.C. Gradually, Chinese society grew more complex. Various groups fought among themselves for land and power.

Warfare in early China was similar to warfare in other ancient societies. Soldiers fought with spears, maces, and bows and arrows. They wore armor made from leather reinforced with metal. Some Chinese armor was made from tough rhinoceros skin. The Chinese even outfitted their horses with armor, which protected them from enemy spears and arrows.

The Chinese began using chariots in battle in the 1200s B.C. Generals used the vehicles as mobile command posts. The general rode in the chariot, along with a drummer, a driver, and archers. The archers defended the chariot with bows and arrows. As the chariot raced from place to place on the battlefield, the general gave orders to the drummer. He pounded out signals on his drum. These signals directed troops on the battlefield.

These bronze figurines from ancient China show soldiers on horseback as well as chariot crews. The Chinese used chariots as early as the 2000s B.C.

ANCIENT GUIDE TO WARFARE

Around 500 B.C., a Chinese general named Sun-tzu wrote a book about military strategy. Called *The Art of War*, it was the first ever military manual. The book includes chapters on fighting on difficult terrain, attacking the enemy, and using spies. It also includes advice on strategy and planning. Sun-tzu offered this and much more advice to other commanders:

- If [your opponent] is taking his ease, give him no rest. If his forces are united, separate them.
- Attack him [the enemy] where he is unprepared, appear where you are not expected.
- Bring war material with you from home, but forage [take food from] on the enemy. Thus the army will have food enough for its needs.
- If you know the enemy and know yourself, you need not fear the result of a hundred battles. If you know yourself but not the enemy, for every victory gained you will also suffer a defeat. If you know neither the enemy nor yourself, you will succumb in every battle.
- Whoever is first in the field and awaits the coming of the enemy will be fresh for the fight; whoever is second in the field and has to hasten to battle will arrive exhausted.
- The spot where we intend to fight must not be made known; for then the enemy will have to prepare against a possible attack at several different points; and his forces being thus distributed in many directions, the numbers we shall have to face at any given point will be proportionately few.

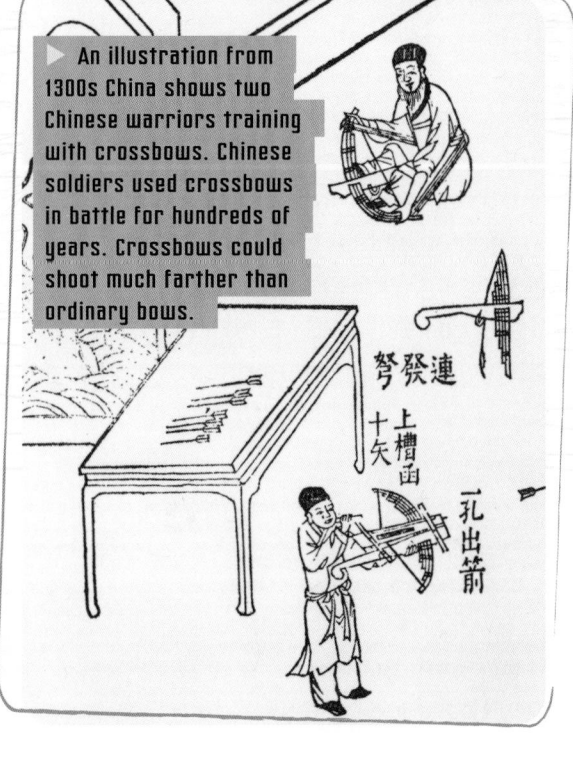

An illustration from 1300s China shows two Chinese warriors training with crossbows. Chinese soldiers used crossbows in battle for hundreds of years. Crossbows could shoot much farther than ordinary bows.

弩發連
上槽面
十矢
孔出箭

THE CROSSBOW

Around 400 B.C., the ancient Chinese made a big step forward in military technology. They invented the crossbow. This was the ancient world's most accurate long-range weapon. The ancient Chinese crossbow was similar to ordinary bows, but it was much more powerful. It was mounted horizontally (crosswise) on a frame. It had a crank or lever for drawing back the bowstring and arrow. An archer didn't have to pull on the string using muscle power alone. The crossbow also had a catch to hold the bowstring in place until the archer was ready to shoot. Bigger, stronger, and steadier than ordinary bows, crossbows could shoot arrows farther and with more force. They could shoot accurately to about 1,320 feet (400 meters).

A GREAT WALL

Emperor Qin Shi Huangdi started construction of the Great Wall of China around 214 B.C. Designed to protect China from northern invaders, the wall was one of the most ambitious military engineering projects in history.

> "To take untaught men to war is called throwing them away."

—Confucius, Chinese philosopher, circa 500 B.C.

▲ The Great Wall of China was originally built to protect China from northern invaders. The wall was built over the course of many centuries and has become a major international tourist site. About 10 million people visit the wall each year.

Workers began by connecting a series of existing walls in the northern part of China. They also built watchtowers along the wall. The towers enabled soldiers to keep guard for invaders.

The wall stood 20 to 30 feet (6 to 9 m) high. It had a road on top, wide enough for five horsemen to ride abreast. If an enemy attacked, Chinese army units could quickly move along the wall and counterattack. Army units camped at the base of the wall. They signaled one another with fires built on top. Later emperors expanded the Great Wall. It eventually stretched about 4,500 miles (7,240 km) east to west across northern China.

TERRA-COTTA WARRIORS

In 1974 farmers in Xi'an, China, made an astounding discovery. When digging a well, they happened into a giant underground pit. The pit contained thousands of life-sized and half-sized terra-cotta (clay) figures.

The farmers had discovered the tomb of Qin Shi Huangdi, the emperor who began construction of the Great Wall of China. The figures were fashioned to look like cavalrymen and foot soldiers. They were placed in the grave to guard Qin Shi Huangdi after death.

Eventually, archaeologists found nearly eight thousand figures in a number of different pits. The figures are incredibly detailed. Their clay clothing and armor are shaped to look just like the real thing. Even the soles of their shoes are adorned with tread patterns. The warriors include different kinds of soldiers: infantrymen (foot soldiers), charioteers, cavalrymen, crossbowmen, and officers. They stand in formation, as if prepared for battle. By studying the figures, archaeologists have learned about Chinese military clothing and operations of the era.

MARTIAL ARTS

The martial arts are ancient Asian combat and self-defense techniques. The earliest form of martial arts, kung fu, developed in China in the 1500s B.C. In kung fu, an unarmed fighter uses the hands and the feet to strike or kick an opponent. In ancient China, warriors used kung fu against enemies. The ancient Chinese also used kung fu as physical and spiritual exercise.

▲ This wall painting of Buddhist monks practising kung fu appears in the Shaolin Monastery in eastern China.

Over the following centuries, Asian people developed many more types of martial arts. Around the world, many modern people practice martial arts for both exercise and self-defense.

▲ The tomb of ancient Chinese emperor Qin Shi Huangdi (259–210 B.C.) contains thousands of terra-cotta soldiers. The terra-cotta army was created to guard the emperor in the afterlife.

In 1998 archaeologists working at the site found another burial pit. This one contained hundreds of small pieces of limestone. Most of the pieces were square or rectangular. Each piece contained tiny holes. Archaeologist realized that the pieces all fit together. By stringing copper wires through the holes, archaeologists fitted the stone pieces together to re-create suits of stone armor and helmets. These objects had not been made for battle. They had been created specially to embellish the emperor's tomb.

CHAPTER FIVE

ANCIENT INDIA

▲ Mohenjo-daro, built around 2600 B.C., was one of the largest settlements of the Indus Valley Civilization. The ruins, discovered in 1922, are located in modern-day Pakistan. Over time, kingdoms in this part of the world expanded by conquering other peoples through warfare.

India's first civilization, the Indus Valley Civilization, flourished from about 2500 to 1700 B.C. A few hundred years later, people from central Asia, took control of India. This group developed a complex culture. They also established two major religions: Buddhism and Hinduism. They created a rich body of art and literature, much of it based on Hindu teaching. Ancient Indian craftspeople produced elaborate jewelry and textiles. Ancient India was also famous for its spices, including pepper, ginger, and cardamom.

In its early years, ancient India didn't have one central government. The territory was made up of many small kingdoms. That started to change in the 500s B.C. In that century, the kingdom of Magadha, in northeastern India, began to conquer other groups. By the 300s B.C., Magadha controlled much of central India.

A man named Candragupta Maurya had bigger ambitions. He overthrew the Magadha ruler in the 320s B.C. He proceeded to conquer most of modern-day India, Bangladesh, and Pakistan. His empire stretched across the Indian subcontinent, from the Bay of Bengal to the Arabian Sea. It grew rich from trade with China and the Middle East.

THE *ARTHASHASTRA*

Historians don't know much about Candragupta, but they knew that during his reign, one of his ministers wrote a book called the *Arthashastra*. The book is a manual on statecraft, or how to run a country. It offers advice on foreign relations, government organization, warfare, law enforcement, economics, and politics. In a chapter on warfare, the *Arthashastra* lists some good times to attack an enemy:

> Or having made the enemy's men sleepless by harassing them at night, he [a commander] may strike them during the day, when they are weary from want of sleep and are parched by heat, himself being under the shade. Or with his army of elephants enshrouded with cotton and leather dress, he may offer a night-battle to his enemy. Or he may strike the enemy's men during the afternoon when they are tired . . . or he may strike the whole of the enemy's army when it is facing the sun.

CHANGE OF HEART

Candragupta's son Bindusara expanded the Mauryan Empire. Bindusara's son Ashoka expanded it even more. In 261 B.C., Ashoka conquered Kalinga, a region in eastern India. The fighting killed more than one hundred thousand people and wounded and displaced many times more.

This lion-crowned pillar in Sarnath, India, is one of many pillars erected by Emperor Ashoka, who ruled India in the 200s B.C. On another pillar, Ashoka denounced warfare.

When Ashoka realized how much suffering the conquest had caused, he became horrified and filled with regret. He renounced war and devoted the rest of his life to Buddhism. Ashoka had a series of proclamations carved on monuments throughout his empire. On one monument, he states his opposition to war:

> On conquering Kalinga the Beloved of the Gods [Ashoka] felt remorse, for when an independent country is conquered, the slaughter, death and deportation of the people is extremely grievous to the Beloved of the Gods and weighs heavily on his mind. . . . This inscription . . . has been engraved so that any sons or great-grandsons that I may have should not think of gaining new conquests. . . . They should only consider conquest by *dhamma* [the teachings of Buddhism] to be true conquest, and delight in *dhamma* should be their whole delight, for this is of value in both this world and the next.

> **"The victory of kings depends mainly upon elephants; for elephants, being of large bodily frame, are [able] . . . to destroy the arrayed army of an enemy, his fortifications and encampments."**
>
> —*Arthashastra,* ancient Indian book on statecraft, 300s B.C.

INDIA'S NOT-SO-SECRET WEAPON

The ancient Indians used the same military technology as other ancient peoples. This technology included bows and arrows, spears, horses, and chariots. But the ancient Indians had something extra. They used elephants in battle. Indian elephants can stand more than 9 feet (3 m) tall and weigh up to 8,000 pounds (3,600 kg). Elephants were bigger and more powerful than anything else on the ancient battlefield. The ancient Indians marched the animals into battle by the hundreds and sometimes the thousands.

▶ This Indian painting shows a war elephant on the battlefield. Armies used male elephants instead of females, because the males were faster and more aggressive. War elephants charged enemy lines, trampled enemy soldiers, and caused enemy horses to stampede.

HUNS AND OTHER HORSEMEN

Central Asia sits north of China, India, and the Middle East. It is a region of vast deserts and grasslands. Throughout ancient times, central Asia was home to nomadic herders. These people traveled with herds of sheep, cattle, camels, and other animals. The central Asians were the first people to breed horses. They were especially skilled on horseback.

Several times in ancient history, central Asian horsemen conquered vast territories and established powerful empires. In about 250 B.C., the Xiongnu people ruled a large empire in east central Asia. People called the Huns lived in west-central Asia. Attila was a Hun leader in the A.D. 400s. He was a fierce horseman who conquered an enormous territory, from Europe in the west to central Asia in the east.

Elephants were versatile military equipment. They could transport soldiers and supplies between battle sites. On the battlefield, they were most often used to charge at the enemy. An elephant charge usually sent enemy soldiers running for their lives. Those who couldn't get out of the way fast enough were trampled. Elephants also terrified enemy horses, which often panicked, reared up, and ran off in the face of approaching elephants.

Soldiers rode on the backs of elephants from big platforms called howdahs. Sometimes several archers rode on a howdah. From this perch, 9 feet (3 m) up, the archers had a superb view of the battlefield and their enemy targets. Sometimes generals rode in howdahs and commanded their soldiers from there.

Elephants have thick hides, which were not easily pierced by ancient weapons. Still, a fast-moving arrow or spear could injure an elephant. So the ancient Indians sometimes outfitted the animals with metal armor, which protected their bodies and legs.

War elephants were unpredictable. When injured or frightened, they often trampled their own armies. Mahouts, or elephant handlers, sometimes had to kill elephants that went out of control. It took an extra-heavy arrow or a sharp steep spike to kill a war elephant.

The ancient Persians learned about war elephants from fighting the ancient Indians. The Persians used their own war elephants against Alexander the Great, a famous Greek general. But even elephants could not stop Alexander's conquest of Persia. Soon elephants became standard military equipment in ancient Europe and the Middle East. One general, Hannibal, marched elephants over the Alps—the largest mountains in Europe—during a war against ancient Rome.

▲ A fifteenth-century edition of Quintus Curtius Rufus's *History of Alexander the Great* includes this illustration of Greek general Alexander facing Indian war elephants.

CHAPTER SIX

THE ANCIENT AMERICAS

▲ The Maya civilization thrived in Mesoamerica (central Mexico and Central America) from about 1000 B.C. to A.D. 900. They built sophisticated cities throughout the region, including Palenque *(above)* in what is now the Mexican state of Chiapas. Life at Palenque included warfare, through which the settlement aimed to maintain and extend its control of people, resources, and land in the area.

Ancient America was home to thousands of different cultures. People lived in the far north, near the North Pole, all the way down to the southernmost tip of South America.

Some ancient Americans were hunter-gatherers. Others were farmers or city dwellers. In modern times, we often use the term *Indian* to refer to all these people. But each group had its own name.

Each group also had its own approach to warfare. Some ancient Americans rarely fought with outsiders. Other groups were more warlike. They fought to acquire new territory and resources. They took prisoners of war as slaves. In Central and South America, several large empires emerged. These empires amassed large armies to defend their territory, conquer new territory, and control conquered peoples.

NORTHERN WARRIORS

Ancient North America did not have empires. Most ancient North Americans lived in small bands, ranging from a few dozen to several hundred people. Most were hunter-gatherers, although some were farmers. Tribes usually had chiefs, but they did not have complex governments. Men of the tribe served as warriors when necessary, but tribes did not have standing, or permanent, armies.

Occasionally ancient North Americans clashed over food, water, or territory. Different tribes sometimes made alliances with one another to fight common enemies. Certain Indian tribes were more warlike than others. The Navajo and the Apache, who lived in the present-day U.S. Southwest, often raided nearby Pueblo Indians. Indians of the Great Plains held warriors in high regard. Plains warriors wore eagle feathers in their hair to mark the killing of enemies.

Like hunter-gatherers in other parts of the world, ancient North Americans fought with spears, clubs, and bows and arrows. In eastern North America, Indians sometimes fought with tomahawks. The tomahawk was similar to an ax. It had a sharp stone blade attached to a wooden handle. Warriors used tomahawks in two ways. Sometimes they simply struck an enemy with a tomahawk. Other times they threw it at the enemy.

This stone tomahawk found in Kentucky would have been used by Native Americans in battle.

PEOPLES OF MIDDLE AMERICA

Ancient Mexico and Central America made up a region called Mesoamerica, which means "middle America." This region was home to a series of ancient cultures—the Olmecs, the Maya, the Toltecs, and the Aztecs. In many ways, these societies were more complex than those of ancient North America. Ancient Mesoamericans constructed temples and monuments, developed systems of writing and mathematics, and built big cities.

Mayan culture flourished in Mesoamerica from about 1000 B.C. to A.D. 900. Archaeologists believe that war was common among the Maya. Mayan cities were surrounded by high walls and deep ditches for defense against attackers. A mural in the ancient Mayan city of Bonampak (in modern-day Mexico) shows Mayan warriors beheading prisoners of war. Ancient Mayan hieroglyphics tell of wars between rival cities.

▼ This section of a mural at the ancient Mayan city of Bonampak (in what is now the Mexican state of Chiapas) shows Mayan warriors, armed with spears, and their seated prisoners. The Mayan style of battle was largely hand to hand, with up-close thrusting and jabbing.

The spear was the Mayan warrior's basic offensive weapon. Maya wall paintings show warriors holding spears, although they also used clubs, battle-axes, and knives. The Maya used obsidian, a glasslike volcanic rock, to make spear tips, axes, knives, and other sharp tools. Weapons with obsidian blades and points were razor sharp and deadly.

▲ The Florentine Codex of the mid-1500s shows Aztecs preparing for a feast to the sun. The figures in this panel hold *macuahuitls*, wooden swordlike weapons embedded with sharp blades of obsidian (a volcanic glass).

EMPIRE

Mayan society declined around A.D. 900. After that the Toltec Empire emerged in Mesoamerica. It lasted for about three hundred years. The next superpower in the region was the Aztec Empire. It emerged in the 1400s and came to dominate Mesoamerica.

The Aztecs had a large army and a large government. It was headed by an emperor and based in the city of Tenochtitlán. This enormous urban center was home to more than two hundred thousand people.

The Aztecs waged war to conquer surrounding territory as well as to take captives. In bloody ceremonies, they sacrificed prisoners of war to their gods. The Aztec warrior's primary weapon was the *macuahuitl*. This was a wooden club lined with sharp pieces of obsidian. Warriors also fought with spears and bows and arrows.

Like other ancient peoples, Aztec warriors used spear-throwers to make their spears travel farther. Called an atlatl, the Aztec spear-thrower was made from a narrow piece of wood or an animal bone. The spear sat in a groove

The atlatl was an Aztec spear-thrower. This view of the back sides of two atlatls shows the grooves into which the spears were placed. The carvings on these atlatls show gods, warriors, and human sacrifice. They are covered in gold.

cut into the top of the device. A hook or a loop of leather held the spear in place. Using an atlatl accurately took practice. The action was like cracking a whip or casting a fishing line. The thrower raised the atlatl overhead and then snapped his throwing arm forward. With an atlatl, a skilled warrior could hurl a spear at more than 100 miles (160 km) per hour.

Aztec warriors wore armor made from thick layers of cotton fabric. This armor offered some protection against spears and arrows. For better protection, the Aztecs sometimes soaked their armor in salty water. When the water dried, it left a hard, salty crust on the fabric, making it harder to cut. Aztec warriors also carried round shields into battle. The shields were made of leather and decorated with colored feathers.

ANOTHER EMPIRE

In the 1400s and 1500s, while the Aztecs dominated in Mesoamerica, the Inca ruled a vast empire in South America. Their capital was in modern-day Cusco, Peru. By conquering some groups and making alliances with others, the Inca came to control a vast stretch of territory along the Pacific coast of South America. It encompassed parts of present-day Colombia, Ecuador, Peru, Bolivia, Chile, and Argentina.

Inca warriors fought with weapons typical of other early peoples. These included slings, bows and arrows, clubs, battle-axes, knives, and spears. Warriors carried shields made of wood or leather. They wore armor made of thick wool or cotton.

OUTMATCHED

In the 1500s, explorers from Europe began to come to the Americas. Spanish explorers traveled through Central and South America, and parts of southern North America. English, Dutch, French, and other Europeans explored North America. The powerful nations of Europe wanted American land, minerals, timber, animal skins and furs, and other rich resources. European governments claimed vast portions of the Americas for themselves.

Sometimes relations between Europeans and Indians were friendly. But more often than not, relations turned violent. European soldiers tried to take American land by force. Indians fought back to defend their ancient homelands.

▶ Mayan warriors typically wore protective items into battle. These included headgear, breastplates, body gear, gauntlets (gloves), and shields. This terra-cotta figure of a Mayan warrior holding a shield dates to A.D. 600–900.

POISON ARROWS

In the modern world, people worry about biological warfare. This involves using harmful microorganisms (germs) against an enemy. Biological warfare is nothing new, however. Ancient peoples used a form of biological warfare thousands of years ago. Ancient archers mixed up secretions from poisonous plants, snake venom, and other toxic substances. They coated arrowheads with poison before doing battle. That way, if an arrow only wounded an enemy, the poison on its tip would still kill him.

Poisonous arrows were common around the ancient world—from Asia to Europe to the Americas. Around the Amazon River in South America, ancient peoples treated their arrows with curare, a poisonous plant extract. Amazonian warriors also used secretions from dendrobatids, commonly known as poison dart frogs *(above)*. Warriors in ancient North America also coated their arrows with plant and animal poisons. Sometimes they used these weapons against European intruders. For instance, a Florida Indian killed Juan Ponce de León, a Spanish explorer, with a poison arrow in 1521.

Although poison arrows were widespread in ancient warfare, they were more commonly used for hunting animals. The same poison that could kill a human enemy also worked against bears, elephants, and much smaller animals.

In many cases, the Indians were stronger in terms of numbers of warriors. They knew the countryside better than their enemies. They used effective guerrilla tactics, such as lightning-quick ambushes. But the Europeans had better weapons. They had gunpowder. This explosive material, which was invented in China, puts the bang into firearms. The Indians had only

> "A very severe conflict ensued, for the enemy [Aztecs] were well provided with bows, arrows, lances [spears] . . . and excellent cotton [body armor]. Besides which they were armed with a species of club . . . and as the ground was strewed with stones they did us much injury with their slings."

—Bernal Díaz del Castillo, Spanish soldier and historian, describing the Spanish conquest of Mexico, 1632

simple weapons made of stone, animal bone, wood, and sometimes metal. In addition, European soldiers rode horses, which were unknown in the Americas until that time.

The combination of firearms and cavalry troops was too much for the Indian defenders. The Aztec and Inca armies fell quickly to Spanish forces. In North America, Indians fought with Europeans in a series of small wars. Some Indians acquired their own firearms and horses, which leveled the playing field somewhat. But for every Indian victory, the Europeans racked up dozens of their own.

CHAPTER SEVEN

ANCIENT GREECE

Ancient Greece is remembered for its great philosophers, playwrights, and scientists. But it is also known for its military achievements. During the 400s B.C., Greek forces defeated the powerful Persian army not once but twice. In the 300s B.C., under the leadership of Alexander the Great, Greece amassed a vast empire. Alexander's forces conquered Persia, Egypt, and parts of central Asia. Greek soldiers used the most advanced weapons of their day. Greek generals developed shrewd battle tactics.

CITY-STATES AT WAR

In its early years, around 800 B.C., ancient Greece was made up of city-states. These political units consisted of a city and the surrounding villages and

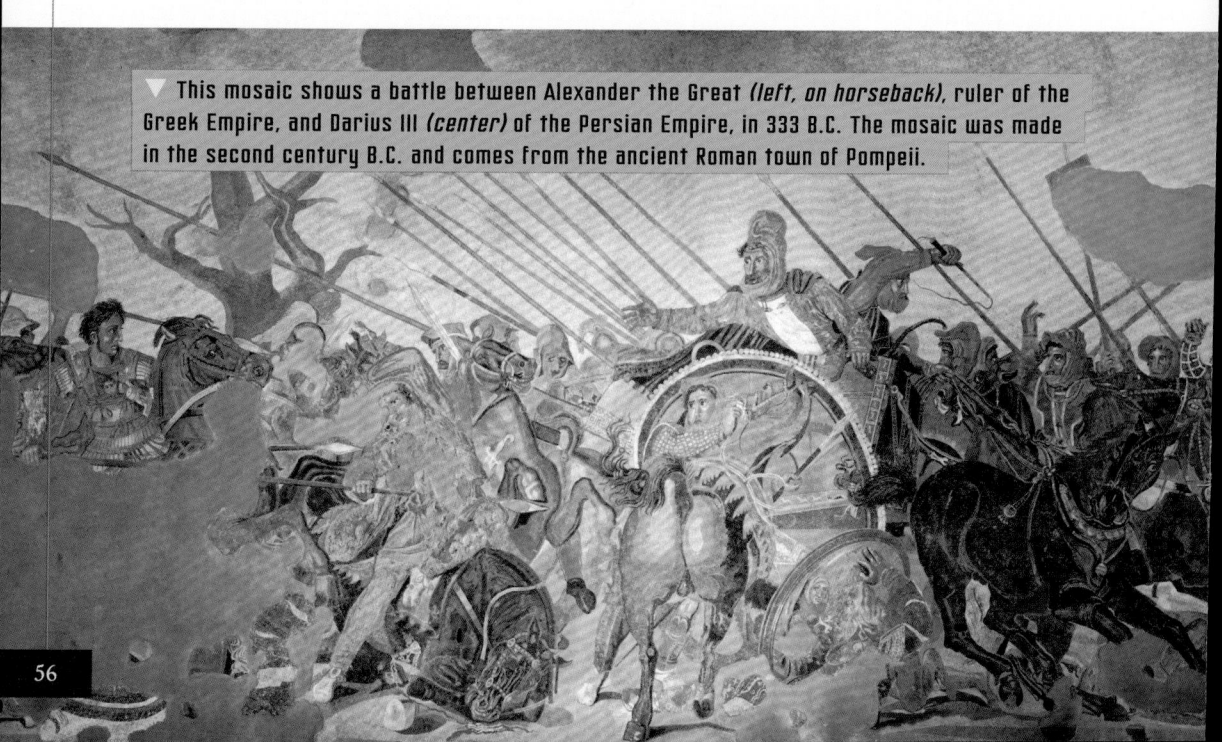

▼ This mosaic shows a battle between Alexander the Great *(left, on horseback)*, ruler of the Greek Empire, and Darius III *(center)* of the Persian Empire, in 333 B.C. The mosaic was made in the second century B.C. and comes from the ancient Roman town of Pompeii.

farms. Each city-state operated like a separate country. It had its own laws, leaders, and army.

Athens and Sparta were the most powerful Greek city-states. They fought each other during the Peloponnesian War (431–404 B.C.). During this conflict, soldiers used tried-and-true weapons such as bows and arrows and spears.

In 424 B.C., the Spartans brought a new weapon to the battlefield. It was an early version of a flamethrower, a weapon that spews out burning liquid or fuel. The Spartans directed their flamethrower at the wooden walls of Delium, an enemy city. The Greek historian Thucydides described the scene:

> The Peloponnesian [Spartan-led] garrison . . . marched against Delium, and attacked the fort, and after [diverse] efforts finally succeeded in taking it by an engine of the following description. They sawed in two and scooped out a great beam from end to end, and fitting it nicely together again like a pipe, hung by chains a cauldron at one extremity [end], with which communicated [connected] an iron tube projecting from the beam, which was itself in great part plated with iron. This they brought up from a distance upon carts to the part of the [city] wall principally composed of vines and timber, and when it was near, inserted huge bellows [air pumps] into their end of the beam and blew with them. The blast passing closely confined into the cauldron, which was filled with lighted coals, sulphur and pitch, made a great blaze, and set fire to the wall, which soon became untenable [unable to be defended] for its defenders, who left it and fled; and in this way the fort was taken.

After many more years of fighting, Sparta finally defeated Athens. Thirty-three years later, the Greek city-state of Thebes conquered Sparta.

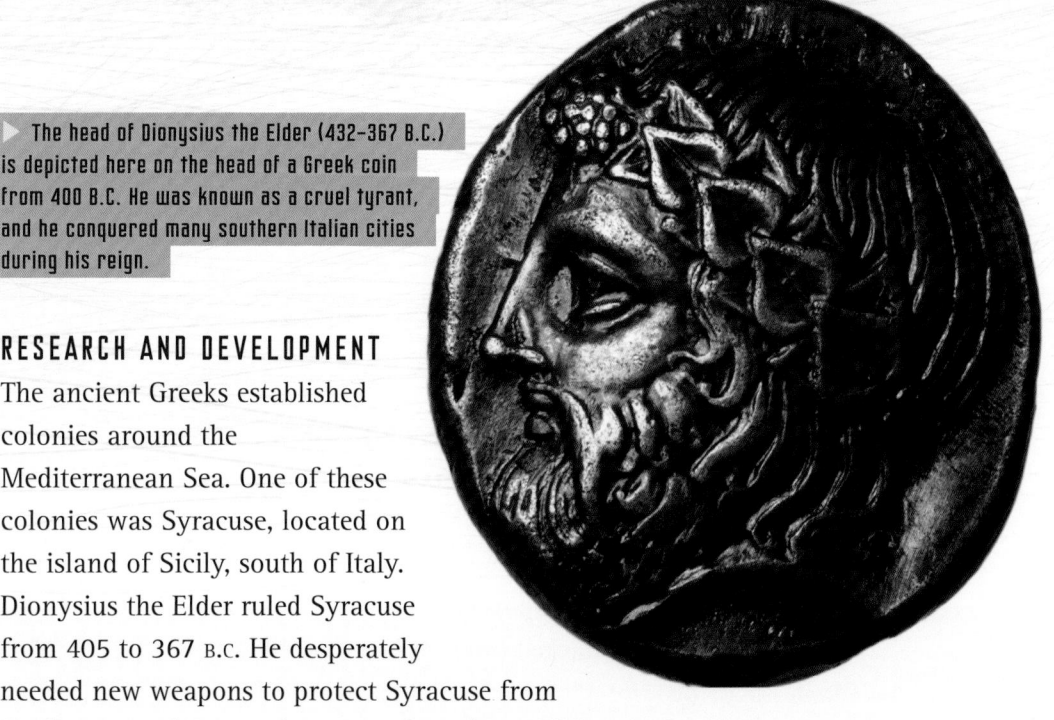

The head of Dionysius the Elder (432–367 B.C.) is depicted here on the head of a Greek coin from 400 B.C. He was known as a cruel tyrant, and he conquered many southern Italian cities during his reign.

RESEARCH AND DEVELOPMENT

The ancient Greeks established colonies around the Mediterranean Sea. One of these colonies was Syracuse, located on the island of Sicily, south of Italy. Dionysius the Elder ruled Syracuse from 405 to 367 B.C. He desperately needed new weapons to protect Syracuse from Carthage, a colony on the coast of northern Africa.

Dionysius wanted a bow that could shoot heavier arrows than handheld bows. He hired engineers and craftspeople and brought them to Syracuse to develop the weapon. He broke the men into teams—much like modern research and development (R&D) teams. He assigned each team one task and set deadlines for meeting goals. Men who met their goals got cash prizes.

Dionysius's R&D wizards invented the *gastraphetes*, or belly bow. The bow was bigger and more powerful than an ordinary bow. It was mounted on a central shaft. An archer braced the shaft against his stomach while pulling the bowstring with both arms. The big bow could shoot a heavy arrow about 990 feet (300 m).

The belly bow was just the start. Greek craftsmen soon developed a belly bow that shot even larger arrows. The bow was too big and heavy for one man to hold. Instead, it sat on a wooden base. To cock the bowstring, the archer turned a winch, or a crank. Each turn of the winch pulled the bowstring back farther and farther, until the bow was ready for firing.

CONQUEROR FROM THE NORTH

Fighting between city-states weakened ancient Greece. Macedonia was a kingdom north of Greece. Its king, Philip II, wanted to expand his territory. He reorganized and enlarged Macedonia's armed forces. Athens and Thebes united to fight Philip, but he quickly defeated them at the Battle of Chaeronea in 338 B.C. Greece became part of the Macedonian kingdom.

One of Philip's most powerful tools was the phalanx. In this infantry formation, soldiers stand shoulder to shoulder and line up several rows deep. The whole block of soldiers advances on an enemy as a unit.

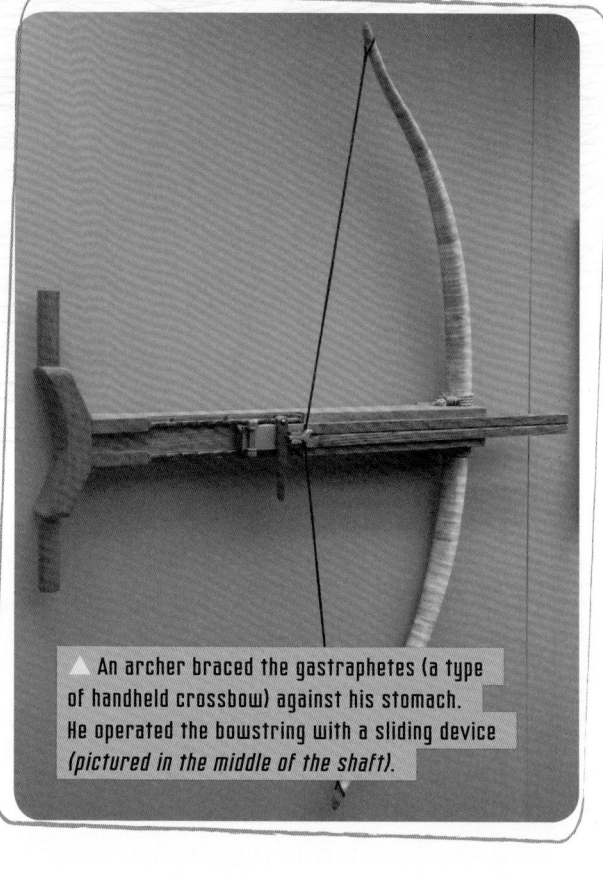

▲ An archer braced the gastraphetes (a type of handheld crossbow) against his stomach. He operated the bowstring with a sliding device (pictured in the middle of the shaft).

Philip's phalanxes were twenty-eight rows deep. The front four rows consisted of 1,024 soldiers armed with bows, spears, and slings. The next sixteen rows contained 4,096 additional soldiers. Those at the front carried spears more than 13 feet (4 m) long. Behind them were men armed with short swords, used for thrusting at close range. Eight lines containing 2,048 soldiers protected the rear of the phalanx. These men carried swords, spears, slings, and other weapons. Each flank (side) of the phalanx was protected by cavalrymen. Philip sometimes combined several phalanxes into a grand phalanx, with up to thirty-two thousand men.

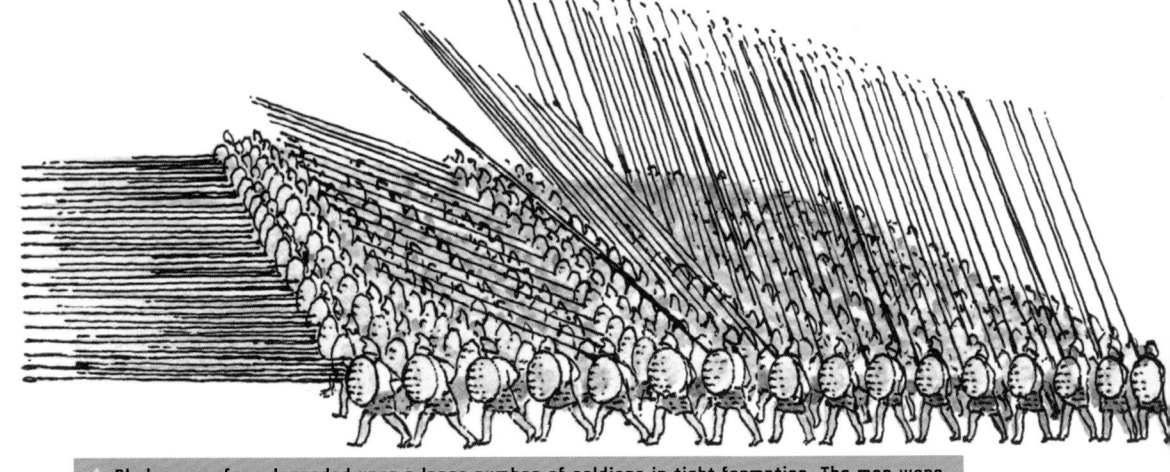

▲ Phalanx warfare depended upon a large number of soldiers in tight formation. The men were armed with spears and swords and protected themselves with heavy, circular shields supported on the shoulder.

At the start of a battle, Philip would order a cavalry charge to break up the enemy ranks. Next, he would order the phalanx itself to charge. The soldiers ran at top speed, staying in formation. The enemy first faced short spears, arrows, and stones, then longer spears, and then thousands of soldiers slashing with swords.

THE *KATAPULTOS*

Military engineers kept improving on the gastraphetes. During Philip's campaigns, his engineers created large machines that could hurl not only

DOUBLE DUTY

Some Greek soldiers carried large rectangular shields. They protected the soldiers from head to legs. The shields were made from wood covered with leather and strengthened with iron. If a man were killed or wounded in battle, his fellow soldiers used his shield as a stretcher. They carried him from the battlefield on his shield.

arrows but also large stones. The Greeks called these devices *katapultos*. We call them catapults.

Ancient catapults were mounted on big wooden frames. A wooden beam held a stone or another ammunition. The beam was attached to twisted bands, made of horsehair, animal tendon, or another stretchy material. The twisted bands stored up energy. When the bands untwisted, they transferred their energy to the beam. It sprang forward and hurled the ammunition through the air.

Catapults revolutionized ancient warfare. An attacking army might mount catapults on tall towers just outside an enemy city. The catapult operators would pummel the city walls with stones or other missiles. The attackers concentrated their firepower on one area of the walls and broke through quickly. In about 200 B.C., a Greek engineer wrote that city walls needed to be at least 15 feet (4.5 m) thick to withstand stones shot from catapults.

▲ Modern-day colored illustrations show what ancient Greek catapults looked like. The mounted beam was able to spring forward to hurl ammunition long distances through the air.

THE TROJAN HORSE

Tricks and hoaxes can be powerful military tactics. The ancient Greeks might have carried out the most famous trick in military history. According to legend, around 1200 B.C., Greek troops besieged the city of Troy, in modern-day Turkey. The siege lasted for ten years without success. Legend tells us that the Greeks tried a new tactic. They sailed away from Troy, leaving behind a huge wooden horse *(below, from a Roman fresco, or wall painting)*. The Trojans believed the horse was a gift to their gods. They dragged it inside the walls of their city. The Trojans then celebrated, believing they had defeated the Greeks.

But the horse was a trick. Greek soldiers were hidden inside it. During the night, the soldiers sneaked out and opened the city gates. The Greek army had not really left Troy. It was waiting offshore. Greek warriors poured in and captured Troy.

Historians don't know how much of the story is true. Many historians think Greece did fight Troy around 1200 B.C. But the story of the Trojan Horse might be pure fiction.

WAR AT SEA

Greece is bordered by water on three sides. It sits on a peninsula that juts into the Mediterranean Sea. It's no wonder, then, that the ancient Greeks were skilled shipbuilders. Greek merchant ships sailed the Mediterranean and nearby seas. The Greeks also developed some of the ancient world's best warships.

The earliest Greek warship was the bireme. *Bi* is Latin for "two." *Reme* comes from the Latin word *remus*, meaning "oar." Biremes had two rows of oars on each side—one row on the ship's upper level and the other on the lower level. The placement was staggered, so that oars weren't positioned directly on top of one another and wouldn't crash into one another. The bireme had a single mast and a sail. Sailors removed the mast during battle. Some biremes were more than 80 feet (24 m) long.

Around 500 B.C., the Greeks began to use triremes. These warships had three rows of oars on each side. The typical ship was about 125 feet (38 m) long and 20 feet (6 m) wide. Trireme crews included about 160 oarsmen,

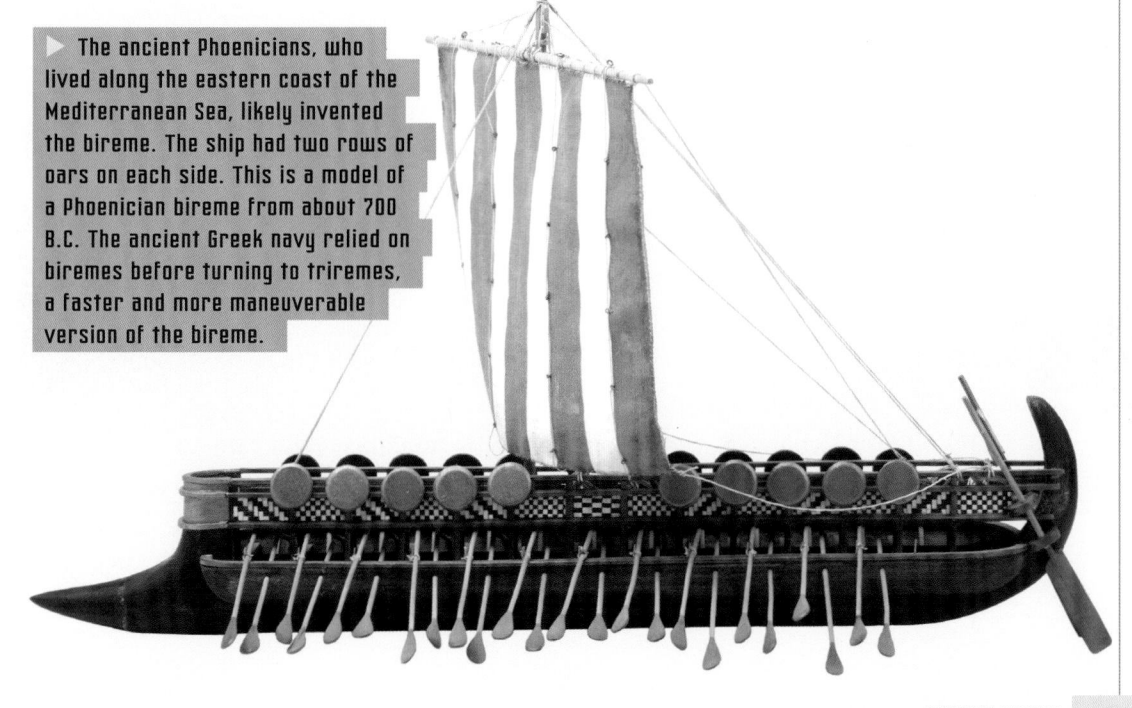

▶ The ancient Phoenicians, who lived along the eastern coast of the Mediterranean Sea, likely invented the bireme. The ship had two rows of oars on each side. This is a model of a Phoenician bireme from about 700 B.C. The ancient Greek navy relied on biremes before turning to triremes, a faster and more maneuverable version of the bireme.

> ## "It is the people who row the ships who give the city [Athens] its power, together with the helmsmen and the rowing masters and . . . officers and the shipwrights [ship builders]."

—Pseudo-Xenophon (the Old Oligarch), an unknown Greek writer, circa 425 B.C.

along with dozens of heavily armed soldiers. The oarsmen propelled the ship at a peak speed of about 8 miles (13 km) per hour.

The Carthaginians, Syracusans, Egyptians, and other ancient peoples also built triremes. Fleets of triremes sailed in formation. When attacking, a group of triremes would maneuver into two columns. Each ship was protected on one side by another ship. The opposite side of the ship was exposed, so the crew could shoot arrows and hurl spears from that side.

FULL SPEED AHEAD

Both biremes and triremes had wooden or metal beaks, or rams, on the front. The beak extended about 10 feet (3 m) in front of the ship's bow. It sat right at the waterline. Sailors used it to smash the hulls of enemy ships.

In the early years of ancient Greek warfare, ships fought at close range. The captain of a bireme or trireme would steer his ship directly into an enemy vessel, ramming it and hoping to tear a hole in its hull. Right after ramming, soldiers from the attacking ship scampered onto the enemy's boat and fought with swords, daggers, and spears.

This situation changed with the invention of catapults. With catapults mounted on deck, ships no longer had to ram an enemy ship to damage it. Soldiers could just launch stones and other missiles from catapults from long distances.

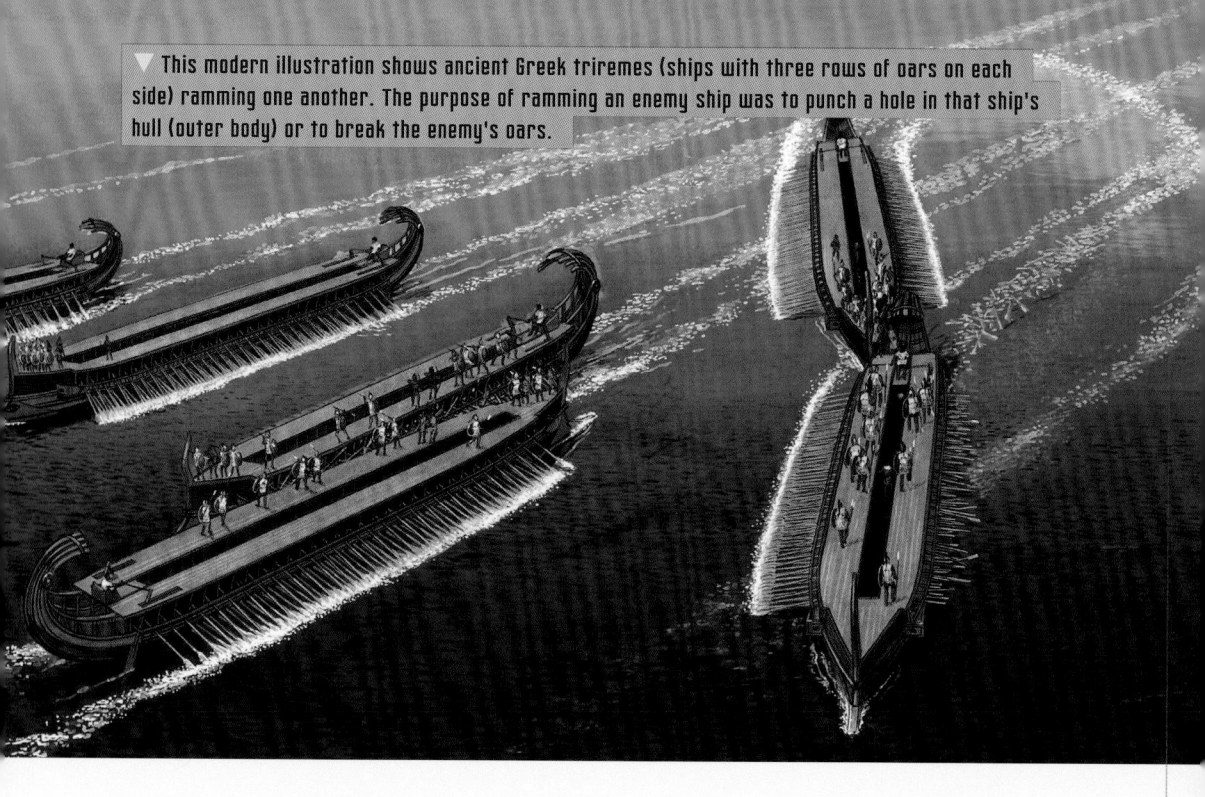

▼ This modern illustration shows ancient Greek triremes (ships with three rows of oars on each side) ramming one another. The purpose of ramming an enemy ship was to punch a hole in that ship's hull (outer body) or to break the enemy's oars.

To carry catapults, ancient navies needed bigger warships. The Greeks built the quinquereme, which was about 150 feet (45 m) long. It still had three levels of oars on each side. But two men pulled each oar on the top two levels, and one man pulled each oar on the bottom level. Later warships were even bigger, with more room for catapults and more men pulling oars.

ARCHIMEDES' CLAW

Archimedes was a Greek engineer who lived in the 200s B.C. He studied physics and mathematics and also invented machines. Archimedes lived in Syracuse. He used his mechanical knowledge to create weapons for the Syracusan army.

Syracuse was a port city. Its walls stood right next to the sea, which made them vulnerable to attack by water. To defend the city against attacking ships, Archimedes created a machine called the Archimedes' Claw.

The claw looked like a modern construction crane. It had one upright beam with a horizontal beam on top. The upright beam stood inside the city

This illustration shows Archimedes' Claws mounted inside the walls of Syracuse. The claws could grab enemy ships and pull them out of the water, smashing the ships and sending sailors to their deaths.

walls. The horizontal beam projected out over the top of the walls, above the sea. A sharp, clawlike hook hung off the beam from the end of a rope. The other end of the rope, behind the city walls, was attached to a team of oxen.

When an enemy ship threatened, Syracusan soldiers readied Archimedes' Claw. When the ship got near enough, soldiers lowered the hook toward the water and snagged the ship's hull with the pointed claw. Behind the city walls, the oxen then pulled the rope, thereby lifting the ship right out of the water. The Greek writer Plutarch, who lived around A.D. 46 to 119, gave this description of Archimedes' invention:

> The ships, drawn by engines within and whirled about, were
> dashed against steep rocks that stood jutting out under the walls,
> with great destruction of the soldiers that were aboard them. A

"A NASTY PRESENT"

Across the ancient world, most soldiers loaded their slings with stones. But the ancient Greeks devised a better missile for slinging. They made bullets by pouring molten (melted) lead into molds. The molds were about 1 inch (2.5 centimeters) across. Lead is denser than stone, so a lead bullet weighs more than a stone of the same size. Because of the extra weight, lead bullets shot from slings did more damage than stones. Molded lead bullets were also more streamlined than stones. They flew straighter and hit their targets with more accuracy. The Greeks sometimes etched insulting messages into the bullet molds. The messages were then imprinted on the bullets. One message said: "A Nasty Present."

ship was frequently lifted to a great height in the air (a dreadful thing to behold) and was rolled to and fro, and kept swinging, until the mariners [sailors] were all thrown out, when at length it was dashed against the rocks, or was let fall.

CHAPTER EIGHT

ANCIENT ROME

▲ The Appian Way *(above)* was a main route for transporting military supplies from ancient Rome to military bases in southern Italy. The first section of the road was completed in the early 300s B.C., and construction to extend the road continued into the 200s B.C.

Ancient Rome traces its beginnings to people called the Latins. Around 2000 B.C., they began grazing herds of sheep in central Italy. By 750 B.C., the Latins had settled into permanent farming villages. One village grew into the city of Rome.

The Romans conquered other groups on the Italian Peninsula. By 264 B.C., Rome ruled all of Italy. Rome fought against Carthage during the Punic Wars, a series of struggles between 264 and 146 B.C. During these wars, Rome conquered additional lands around the Mediterranean Sea, including Spain and Greece. The empire continued to expand. By the second century A.D., Rome controlled much of Europe, the Middle East, and northern Africa.

MAINTAINING AN EMPIRE

To defend its empire, ancient Rome built a strong army. The principal military unit was the legion. During the reign of Emperor Augustus, from 27 B.C. to A.D. 14, Rome had almost thirty legions. At this time, each legion consisted of six thousand men. Legions were divided into smaller units called cohorts, each with four hundred men. Cohorts were broken down further into centuries, groups of one hundred men. An officer called a centurion led each century. Soldiers usually enlisted in the Roman legions for twenty years.

To quickly transport troops and weapons, the Romans built more than 50,000 miles (80,000 km) of roads. These connected all parts of the vast empire. Roman roads were built to last. They had sturdy stone foundations up to 5 feet (1.5 m) thick. They were paved with blocks of cut stone.

Roman legions built *castra*, or military camps, throughout their empire. Camps were built according to a standard plan. They had two main streets that crossed in the center of camp. A wall surrounded the camp, and a ditch surrounded the wall. Some castra were temporary. They were used for only

◀ Ancient Roman military camps were called castra. Shown here are the ruins of an ancient Roman castra located in modern Romania. It served as a military camp between A.D. 166 and 274.

a few weeks or a few months. Others were more permanent military bases. They served as headquarters for long-term military campaigns.

DRESSED FOR BATTLE

Military uniforms varied over the years of ancient Roman history. And different kinds of soldiers (archers, officers, and so on) wore different kinds of uniforms. But the typical Roman foot soldier wore a tunic—a belted, knee-length garment. He wore metal armor across his chest and stomach. He also wore greaves, or shin armor, and a metal helmet. A round or rectangular shield gave him additional protection from incoming stones, arrows, spears, and dagger thrusts.

The soldier's combat boots were well designed for support, comfort, and protection. The boots looked like modern leather sandals. They were open-toed, with laces at the ankle. The upper portions of the boots were webbed, which allowed them to flex as soldiers marched. The openings in the leather also allowed the boots to dry quickly after marches in wet weather. The soles were made from single pieces of leather. Iron nails pounded into the soles acted like cleats on modern athletic shoes. The nails improved traction and helped reduce wear on the soles.

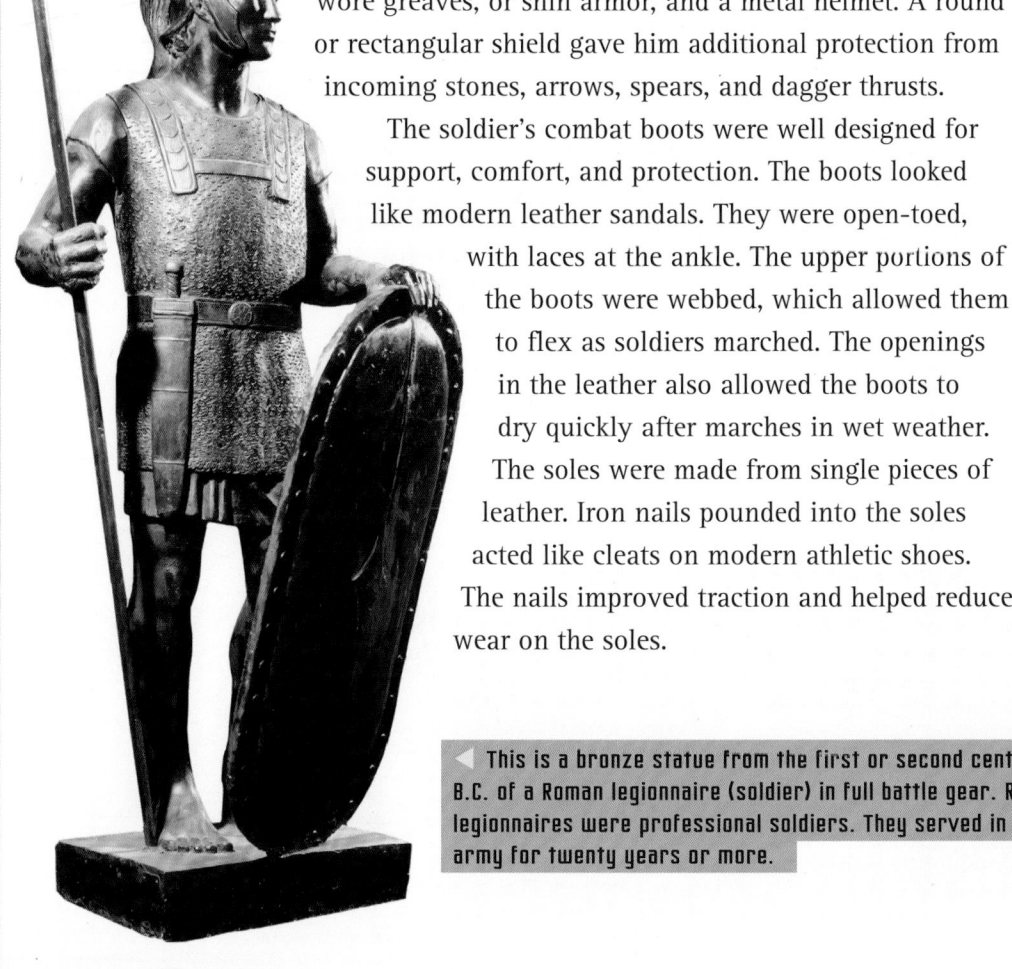

◄ This is a bronze statue from the first or second century B.C. of a Roman legionnaire (soldier) in full battle gear. Roman legionnaires were professional soldiers. They served in the army for twenty years or more.

ROMAN BRITAIN

Roman general Julius Caesar invaded Britain in 55 B.C. but was not able to conquer the territory. In A.D. 43, Roman armies again invaded Britain and this time succeeded. Modern-day England and Wales became part of the Roman Empire.

The Romans built towns, temples, government offices, public baths, roads, and forts throughout their British territory. In the north, near the border with modern-day Scotland, Roman soldiers built Hadrian's Wall *(right)*, named for the Roman emperor. The wall was designed to protect Roman Britain from the Scots and Picts, warlike peoples from the north. It ran for 73 miles (117 km) across northern England.

Britain remained a Roman province for more than three hundred years. But as the Roman Empire declined in the A.D. 300s, Rome struggled to protect Britain from outside invaders. Finally, Roman troops left Britain to defend other parts of the empire. Scots and Picts then invaded Britain, followed by Angles, Saxons, and Jutes from the European mainland. By the end of the A.D. 500s, Britain was under Anglo-Saxon (Angle and Saxon) control.

ROMAN ARTILLERY

Roman legions used catapults for hurling stones, arrows, and other objects at enemies. The most powerful Roman catapult could hurl a 55-pound (25 kg) rock more than 1,320 feet (400 m).

The onager was a small Roman catapult. Armies used it to fire medium-sized stones. *Onager* is also the name of an Asian

▲ Ancient Roman armies used the onager, a type of catapult, for attacking forts and settlements.

wild ass. The Romans used the same name for their small catapults because they "kicked" stones with plenty of power, just like the kick of an angry ass. Onagers were easier to build than larger catapults and easier to move from place to place. Onagers eventually replaced larger catapults in the ancient Roman arsenal.

But even onagers were heavy and difficult to transport. They were not practical for the fast-paced action of battle. Romans used them mainly during sieges. Just before the first century A.D., the Roman army began using smaller, more mobile catapults. They could be moved easily and shot from the battlefield. Each Roman legion traveled with about thirty small catapults, as well as soldiers who specialized in shooting and maintaining them. In battle, catapult operators attacked the enemy with small catapults from a distance before the infantry attacked at close range.

During the second and third centuries A.D., Roman engineers developed several new kinds of artillery (large guns). The *cheiroballista* was a small

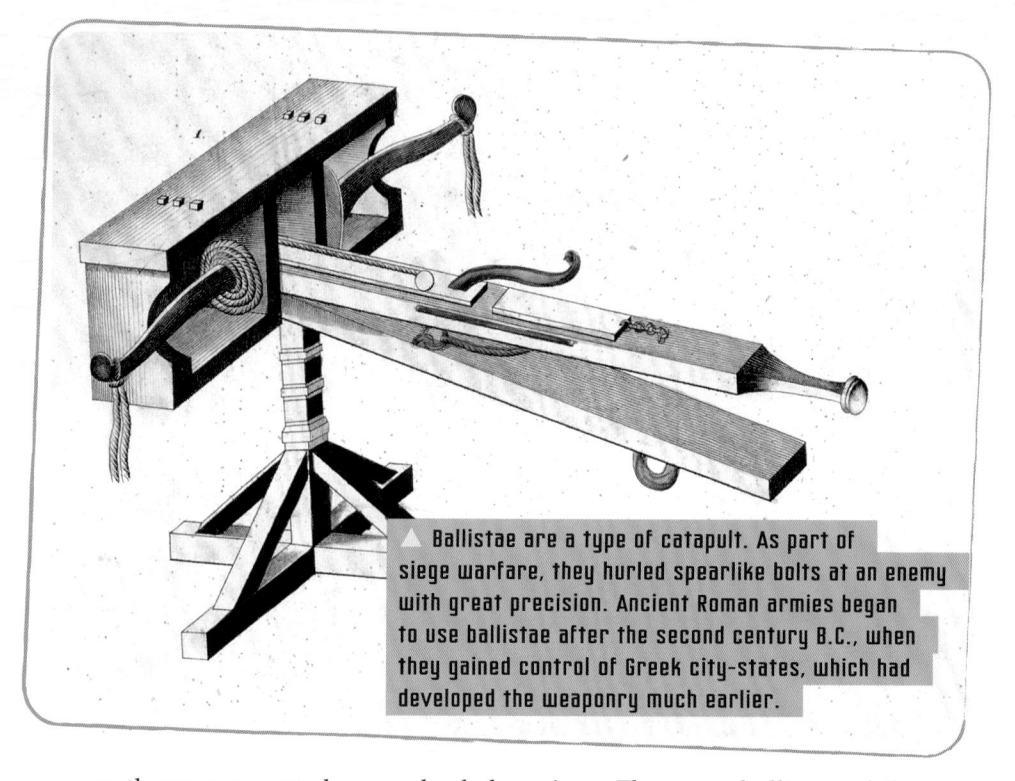

▲ Ballistae are a type of catapult. As part of siege warfare, they hurled spearlike bolts at an enemy with great precision. Ancient Roman armies began to use ballistae after the second century B.C., when they gained control of Greek city-states, which had developed the weaponry much earlier.

arrow thrower mounted on a wheeled carriage. The *manuballista* and the *arcuballista* were similar, but they had no carriages. They were handheld arrow shooters, similar to crossbows.

THE TESTUDO

When marching toward the enemy, the ancient Romans sometimes used a clever technique. Foot soldiers organized themselves into a formation called a testudo. The men lined up in rows, three or more rows deep. The soldiers in the first row held their shields in front of them. The men in the following rows held their shields above their heads. The men on the ends of rows held their shields out to the side. The edges of the shields overlapped or had very little space between them. Thus the soldiers marched inside something like a big metal box. Enemy stones, spears, and arrows would hit the shields and bounce off, rarely getting through to the men inside. *Testudo* is the Latin word for "tortoise." The men in a testudo moved inside a protective shell, much like a tortoise beneath its shell.

The Roman general Mark Antony used testudos when he invaded Parthia, a kingdom in central Asia, in 36 B.C. The first-century Greek writer Plutarch described the formation:

> Then the shield-bearers wheeled about, enclosing the lighter armed troops within their ranks, while they themselves dropped on one knee and held their shields out before them. The second rank held their shields out over the heads of the first, and the next rank likewise. The resulting appearance is very like that of a roof, affords a striking spectacle [sight], and is the most effective of protections against arrows, which glide off from it.

▼ This modern reenactment of ancient Roman warfare shows the testudo, or tortoise, formation. Typically, soldiers in the front positioned their shields in front of their bodies. Men in the back rows lifted their shields above their heads to protect the formation from above. If necessary, the soldiers on the flanks (sides) would use their shields to protect their bodies from the side.

WOMAN WARRIOR

Since ancient times, war has primarily been a male pursuit. But women warriors are not unknown. One example is Boudicca *(below right)*, an ancient British queen. In about A.D. 60, after her husband died, she led a British rebellion against the Roman governor of Britain. The rebellion was spurred by the governor's brutal treatment of Boudicca's people. The Roman historian Tacitus described Boudicca standing in her chariot, addressing her soldiers before battle. "On this spot we must either conquer, or die with glory," she told them. "There is no alternative . . . my resolution is fixed."

Boudicca's troops defeated a Roman legion and attacked the Roman-British city of London. But the Romans eventually defeated her. She killed herself by taking poison rather than be captured.

BUILDING BETTER WARSHIPS

Like other ancient peoples, the Romans sometimes fought at sea. They used triremes and quinqueremes, based on Greek designs. But the Romans also improved on the designs. Roman ships had thicker, stronger gunwales (upper edges) than did Greek ships. The gunwales could better withstand ramming by an enemy ship. Roman ships also had heavier, stronger beaks than did Greek ships. These beaks were better for smashing through the hulls of enemy vessels. Some Roman warships had fighting towers. These were elevated platforms from which archers shot arrows at enemy sailors.

The bireme *(right)* and the *liburnian* were two types of ships that each had two rows of oars on each side. The liburnian, however, was lighter and faster than the bireme and became a key ship in the Roman navy's fleet in the first century B.C.

During the First Punic War (264–241 B.C.), the Romans introduced a new device to warships. Called the *corvus*, it was a narrow wooden plank, about 18 feet (5 m) long. It had a heavy metal spike attached to one end. Before or after a fight, the corvus stood upright near the bow of the Roman warship. Ropes held it in place. But when an enemy warship got close enough, sailors let the corvus come crashing down. The spiked end hit the enemy deck. The spike dug into the deck and held tight. Then Roman sailors swarmed across the corvus and onto the enemy ship, where they fought with the enemy hand to hand.

LEARNING FROM PIRATES

In ancient times, pirates prowled the Mediterranean and other seas. They attacked merchant ships and stole their valuable cargo. On the Mediterranean, pirates traveled in small, fast, easy-to-maneuver ships called uniremes. They had one row of oars on each side.

At the same time, the Roman navy sailed in triremes and quinqueremes. These ships were big, heavy, and slow. They were great for ramming enemy warships. But they weren't fast or easy to handle. Roman military engineers wanted a sleeker, lighter warship for maneuvering in sea battles and for chasing down enemies. They saw the advantages of pirate ships and copied the design.

"Veni, vidi, vici" ["I came, I saw, I conquered"]

—Roman general Julius Caesar, on his victory over Pharnaces II, the king of Pontus, 47 B.C.

Instead of uniremes, with one row of oars per side, the Romans built liburnians. These warships had two rows of oars per side. They were light and fast but still had plenty of power. By the first century A.D., the liburnian had become the main Roman warship.

DECLINE AND FALL

Maintaining the enormous Roman Empire wasn't easy. Enemies were constantly active on the edges of Roman territory. Germanic tribes attacked in the north. Parthian forces attacked from the east. At the same time, Roman noblemen fought among themselves for the title of emperor of Rome. Some men seized power by force. Amid the political chaos, in the A.D. 200s, Roman institutions began to break down. The Roman army steadily weakened. Its soldiers became less disciplined and less skillful.

In the A.D. 300s, the empire split into eastern and western halves. The Eastern Roman Empire set up a new capital in Turkey. The eastern empire grew larger and stronger. But in the west, the chaos continued.

Around A.D. 390, a wealthy Roman named Flavius Vegetius Renatus wrote a book about Roman military practices. Called *On Military Affairs*, this book described the Roman legions of earlier centuries. It discussed the training and discipline of soldiers, the organization of military units, the responsibilities of officers, and battle tactics and strategy. Vegetius said that the Roman Empire could restore its strength by returning to its earlier military glory.

But it was too late for ancient Rome. The empire grew weaker and weaker. The Roman army was stretched too thin to defend all parts of the empire. One Germanic group invaded Roman-held Spain and North Africa. Another attacked the city of Rome itself. Finally, in A.D. 476, the Germanic leader Odoacer captured Rome. With this event, the Roman Empire came to an end.

AFTER THE ANCIENTS

After Rome fell to invaders, Europe entered a period called the Middle Ages (during the years 500 to 1500). Many small kingdoms emerged in Europe during this era. Kings and noblemen amassed armies and fought one another for power and territory.

The Middle Ages are sometimes called the Dark Ages, because art, culture, and learning were minimal in Europe during these years. Few Europeans went to school. Few craftspeople knew about or improved upon ancient technology. But people of the Middle Ages didn't forget about ancient times. European kings were particularly interested in the warfare of ancient Rome. Scribes, or writers, made copies of Vegetius's *On Military Affairs*. Kings and other rulers studied the book to learn all they could about organizing their armies and outwitting their enemies.

Weapons did not change much during the early Middle Ages. Soldiers continued to fight with bows and arrows, catapults, and other weapons developed in ancient times. For protection against invaders, rulers built strong castles. These fortifications had high stone walls, watchtowers, drawbridges, moats, and other defensive features. Castles also served as homes for rulers and their families, headquarters for kingdoms, and bases of operations for military campaigns.

BANG, BANG

Midway through the Middle Ages, military technology changed dramatically. Around A.D. 900, Chinese inventors learned to combine saltpeter, charcoal, and sulfur to make gunpowder. This explosive material can propel a bullet or a cannonball with great speed and force. The Chinese first used gunpowder in small cannons. The technology spread from China to the Middle East to Europe.

After cannons, military engineers applied gunpowder technology to handheld firearms, such as muskets and rifles. Warfare had always been deadly. But gunpowder made it even deadlier and more destructive. Cannonballs could knock down castle walls. Bullets shot from handheld firearms could pierce metal armor.

An Indian illustration from the 1500s shows Indian soldiers using guns and bombards (a type of cannon) in battle. Bullets and cannonballs were far more powerful than arrows and other early missiles.

THE BUSINESS OF WAR

By the 1500s, Europe was home to large, powerful states. These included France, Britain, and Spain. Like the ancient empires before them, these nations needed strong armies and navies. Equipped with firearms and cannons, as well as tried-and-true technology such as horses, swords, and daggers, European soldiers battled one another. They also conquered territories in Asia, Africa, and the Americas.

In the 1700s and 1800s, the Industrial Revolution occurred in Europe. During this era, people invented new machines, such as steam engines. They developed railroads and other transportation systems. The new technology wasn't created specifically for warfare. But people quickly realized that the new machines had great military benefits. For instance, trains could move an army in a few hours much farther than men marching on foot could travel in days. And soldiers transported by train arrived at the battlefield rested and ready to fight.

In the early 1900s, new inventions kept coming—and military leaders kept incorporating them into their battle plans. Officers used telephones and radios to communicate with one another. They used gasoline-powered trucks to carry troops and equipment. They used airplanes to spy on and shoot at the enemy from above. Some new inventions were specifically made for the military. These included tanks, fighter planes, machine guns, and submarines.

WORLD WAR

By the time of World War I (1914–1918), warfare was becoming more mechanized. No one fought with bows and arrows anymore. Armies assailed the enemy with rifles, machine guns, tanks, and big artillery pieces.

World War II (1939–1945) saw the introduction of additional technology. One example is radar. This device uses radio waves to track moving or hard-to-see objects. During World War II, armies used radar to track enemy ships and planes. The atomic bomb was the most destructive military technology ever used. The United States used this weapon at the end of World War II. It dropped atomic bombs on Hiroshima and Nagasaki, two Japanese cities, in 1945. The explosions destroyed the cities and killed tens of thousands of people.

MODERN TIMES

Modern warfare bears little resemblance to warfare of ancient times. In the twenty-first century, warfare is high tech to the extreme. Armies study

▲ An operations specialist views a radar screen aboard the USS *Fife*. Radar equipment sends out pulses of radio waves, which bounce off any objects in their way. When the waves bounce back, they are picked up and turned into imagery that can be seen onscreen. Modern armies can track enemy aircraft, ships, guided missels, and more via radar.

enemy positions using satellite photographs, which are taken from spacecraft. Soldiers set off explosives by remote control. They use robots to diffuse bombs. Laser beams guide bombs and other missiles precisely to their targets. Armies even operate in cyberspace. They hack into one another's computers to steal military secrets.

Does all this new technology make ancient warfare technology obsolete? Do we have nothing left to learn from ancient warriors? Modern military leaders would be quick to answer no. At the United States Military Academy, which trains U.S. army officers, students still read Sun-tzu's *The Art of War*. They also study Vegetius's *On Military Affairs*. Modern officers find that much ancient military advice still rings true many centuries later.

Many ancient tactics—such as guerrilla warfare and siege warfare—are still used in modern times. In fact, guerrilla warfare might be the tactic of the future. In the twenty-first century, armies often find themselves fighting against terrorists. These groups use guerrilla tactics, such as small bombings, to frighten and harm their enemies. They don't dress in military uniforms and are often hard to distinguish from civilians. In response, large armies have to use guerrilla tactics of their own. For instance, the modern U.S. military trains soldiers to fight in small groups and to carry out quick ambushes—much like the ancient Scythians did thousands of years ago.

A PASSION FOR THE PAST

Many modern people are fascinated with ancient warfare. They study old battles, ancient weapons, and ancient armor and uniforms. Some people take this fascination one step further. They dress up like warriors from ancient Rome, Greece, and Sumer. They make sure their uniforms and weapons are historically accurate—right down to the laces on their boots and the points on their spears. They even reenact ancient battles—although no one really gets hurt.

The Legio VI Victrix is one of many ancient military reenactment groups active in the United States. Based in Los Angeles, California, this group models itself on a Roman garrison stationed in Britain in the second century A.D. Members gather once a month to march and drill. They perform at historical fairs and other special events. Several times, Hollywood has come calling. For instance, in 2002, when the producers of the movie *Kingdom of David* needed actors to play ancient Roman soldiers, they hired Legio VI Victrix. In March 2010, reenactors from all over the United States gathered in Arkansas, for a full-scale reenactment of the Roman invasion of Britain in A.D. 43. Some reenactors dressed like Roman soldiers. Others dressed like the British tribesmen who opposed the invasion.

ANCIENT WAR MACHINES COME TO LIFE

People are also fascinated with ancient war machines. Modern engineers have reproduced ancient-style catapults according to the original plans. One reproduction onager could throw 10-pound (4.5 kg) stones the length of three football fields. Another reproduction catapult fired an arrow into a target and then fired another arrow that split the first one in two.

In the mid-1980s, British historians built a full-sized trireme based on ancient pictures and texts. Called the *Olympias*, the boat is 131 feet (40 m) long and 20 feet (6 m) wide. It has seats for 170 rowers, 85 per side, on three levels. It also has two sails. Project leaders tested the *Olympias* at sea six times between 1987 and 1994. Each time, organizers recruited 170 volunteers to pull on the oars. Everyone pulling together got the ship moving at a speed of 9 knots—a little faster than 9 miles (14 km) per hour. The ship also proved very easy to maneuver.

THE LESSONS OF WAR

War is never pretty, and it's always tragic. It always involves death and destruction. However, soldiers sometimes go to war for noble purposes—such as to defeat a cruel dictator or to free enslaved peoples. In those cases, war can be a positive.

War has changed the course of human history, and by studying war, we can find out about the past. By studying ancient military technology, we can learn even more. Ancient warfare combines many other technologies, such as machinery, construction, communications, and transportation. So when we study ancient warfare technology, we are really learning about ancient society as a whole. It is a lesson worth learning.

TIMELINE

CA. 8000 B.C.   A massacre with bows and arrows takes place at Jebel Sahaba in modern-day Sudan. Jericho, the first known walled city, is built in modern-day Israel.

CA. 5000 B.C.   People in the Middle East begin using copper to make tools and weapons.

CA. 3100 B.C.   Upper Egypt conquers Lower Egypt, and the two kingdoms unite.

CA. 3000 B.C.   People in the Middle East begin making tools and weapons from bronze. People in the Middle East start to use wheels in both transportation and warfare.

1500s B.C.   Kung fu develops in China.

CA. 1550 B.C.   Hittites invade Mesopotamia. They use iron weapons, which give them the advantage in battle.

1400s B.C.   Thutmose III of Egypt conquers Megiddo and other parts of modern-day Syria and Israel.

CA. 1270 B.C.   Ramses II of Egypt and Hattusilis III, king of the Hittites, sign the earliest known peace treaty.

CA. 1200 B.C.   According to legend, the Trojan War takes place in ancient Turkey.

513 B.C.   The Persian emperor Darius invades Scythian territory, but Scythian guerrilla attacks turn back his forces.

CA. 500 B.C.   Sun-tzu writes *The Art of War*, the world's first military manual. The ancient Greeks begin using triremes in sea battles.

480 B.C.   The Persian emperor Xerxes builds a bridge of boats across the Hellespont to invade Greece.

431–404 B.C.   The Greek city-states of Athens and Sparta fight one another during the Peloponnesian War.

CA. 400 B.C.   The ancient Chinese invent the crossbow. Greek engineers invent the gastraphetes, or belly bow.

338 B.C.   Philip of Macedonia defeats Athens and Thebes at the Battle of Chaeronea. Greece becomes part of Philip's empire.